T.W. JOHNSON

GOD LOVES THE COMMON PERSON

In God's love
Terry Johnson

GOD LOVES THE COMMON PERSON
Author: T. W. Johnson
Cover Artist: David G. Danglis

Contact: pastortwj@yahoo.com

ISBN: 978-1-935018-10-0
Five Stone Publishing
493 Republic Street
Potter, Kansas 66002 all rights reserved
©Copyright T.W.Johnson 2009

Please email T.W. Johnson at: pastortwj@yahoo.com for republication permission.

Table of Contents

Introduction --- 5
Now For The Rest of the Story --- 9
Today Was Going To Be The Day --- 19
To Have The Faith Of A Child --- 31
The Enforcer Falls --- 44
Did You Listen To Your Son Last Night? --- 58
Hey! I Want To Talk To You --- 70
Jesus Is Alive --- 88
I Must Be The Best --- 102
He Will Love Me Or Else --- 112
Will You Trust Me --- 125
I Want All Of You, Lord --- 142
Lord, I Want My Family To Know You --- 154
What An Awesome God You Are --- 175
No, You Just Don't Understand --- 184
Conclusion --- 196

Introduction

The morning broke beautiful. The bright sun, the sky alive with white fluffy clouds, and a crisp chill in the air heralded the fact that winter was once more upon us. It does not seem possible that so many years have come and gone. It seems like yesterday that I heard the cry of my firstborn child, and yet I recently crossed the threshold of welcoming my great-granddaughter into the world. Four generations have flowed out of my mother's womb. So many stories to tell. So many good times line the path I have walked, laced with a fair amount of challenges, dressed with a number of disappointments, punctuated with outright failures, spiced with dramatic recoveries, and topped with a helping of delightful victories. Sound familiar? I do not pretend to be unique, although the Apostle Peter in I Peter 2:9 would have you know that I am peculiar. I cannot claim to hold an advantage with God over anyone.

For forty years I rose early in the morning, performed my daily ritual of showering and shaving, drove to a very impressive building, punched a time clock, fulfilled my obligation of employment, and waited patiently for Saturday to come. Fortunately, for the last two years, every day has been a Saturday. Retirement is awesome; however, that still does not make me special or unique. I have had the great privilege of loving and living with a tremendous woman for the last 45 years. Together we have enjoyed watching our three children grow, leave home, and begin families of their own. Many might say that I have been very fortunate to have lived what they refer to as the great American dream; however, that still does not make me special or unique. If I were one of many in a great crowd of people, the odds are you would not be able to recognize me. Matter of fact, if I was in a small group of people, you would have a difficult time picking me out unless you made a lucky guess. You see, I am simply that common individual who, over the course of my life, has met many wonderful people who have entered my life, left part of themselves in me, taken part of me, and then, like the wind, had gone elsewhere. I never was that hero type who scored the winning basket in the crucial game, or drove in the winning run against our arch rival, or ran the fastest mile, or climbed the highest mountain, or closed the mega deal that made the company millions.

Does that bother me? No! I stand here amazed (actually I am sitting), questioning why my Lord would ask me to write a book. Now I realize that questioning God can be a risky proposition. However, there surely must be those more learned and qualified than I. Surely there are many well-known authors whose works have impacted thousands of readers who can express themselves better than I can. Surely there are great scholars who have spent a lifetime studying and who understand the Hebrew and Greek languages well enough to articulate the great mysteries of God much better than I can. Surely there are many great and well known pastors, both men and women, who have faithfully developed wonderful, energetic churches who are better qualified to speak for God than I am. Surely these individuals would be more homiletically sound, or exegetically qualified to write a book than I am. You see, I am just an ordinary "Joe".

"Yes, I know," came that still small voice, "and that is exactly what I want. The only qualifications I need are these," He said. " Do you love Me?"

"Why, yes, Lord, You know that I love you with everything I am."

"Do you trust Me?"

"Lord, You know that I trust You with everything I have."

"Then simply do as I ask for there are many who need to know and understand that simple truth you experienced so many years ago."

Needless to say, this book has flowed out of a willingness to be obedient to what my Lord wants me to do. Therefore, I trust and believe that these simple stories and accounts of how God has moved in my life, in the lives of my family, and in the lives of the special people I am about to introduce you to, will stir something in your heart that will draw you into a vibrant, life-changing relationship with the personal, wonderful, forgiving, loving, caring, living Savior who wants everyone to understand that . . .

God loves the common person!

Now for the Rest of the Story

That brings us to the immortal words of legendary commentator Paul Harvey, "and now for the rest of the story." Well, not quite yet. That may be where I would like to start; however, that would not do justice to what the Lord wants to accomplish. You see, I need to go back to the beginning. Not the crawling, bawling, dirty diaper beginning, but back to a period in my life when everything around me was collapsing. I had spent several years building a small empire. I had everything I needed and most of what I wanted. I had money, power, and recognition. We were living in a huge home in the heart of the country club in a small town in central Illinois. I was close to completing two other very nice homes in the same area. I also had a lot overlooking a small lake upon which I was going to build my dream home. I had an option on sixteen acres of land in the fastest growing commercial section of town upon which sixty-four apartment units, a convenience-type store and a laundromat were to be built. I had accomplished all this while working full-time and going to college in the evenings.

The sky was blue, the birds were singing, and everything was "hunky-dory". That was until a severe storm arose on the horizon. Those who have come to the startling realization that Social

Security and Medicare are right around the corner may remember a time in the early '70s when the US economy not only went sour but almost collapsed. Interest rates shot up to 22 percent, inflation was rampant, long lines of cars blocked traffic as they waited in line for what little gasoline there was. Unemployment skyrocketed and the housing industry literally collapsed. Needless to say, I had a problem, Houston!

I was sitting on one half million dollars in real estate that was not completed. I did not have enough money to complete the houses under construction, and no one was willing to lend money against the equity in them. My employer was forced to lay me off. There was no work, which meant I was forced to leave town in order to earn money just to cover our living expenses. It was the middle of February and it was very cold. The propane company threatened to remove their tank because I could not pay them. I was working two hours from home and became desperately sick. If there was anyone who could sympathize with Job, I could. I was forced to quit my job. I loaded up my tools and started for home. That is when things became slightly bizarre. I have no idea how I got home. The first thing I recall after leaving work is standing in my bedroom and yet I was not there. I was outside of the house looking through a second story window watching myself lose my mind. Do I expect you to believe that. I am not sure I can myself because I do not understand it either. I was freaking out when my wife came into the room. I do not know what she saw, however, she screamed and slapped me and said "snap out of it". Instantly I was back in the room standing next to her. Needless to say I was definitely frightened, confused, and bewildered. Those things simply don't happen, or do they?

It was obvious that something had to be done. The next morning I visited a good friend who happened to be an attorney. After reviewing the situation and looking at the alternatives, it became apparent the only option that made sense was the dreaded "B" word. Now for someone who took great pride in what he had accomplished, even to the point of great arrogance, bankruptcy was like a dagger in the heart. All the hard work, all the hopes and dreams and promises, the big home, the fancy cars, the prestige, and the networking with the movers and shakers was about to disappear in a puff of smoke. For ten years I had literally ignored my family for the sake of a selfish desire to "be somebody". I do not understand why my wife tolerated what I put her through. She literally had to raise our three sons by herself and yet she stayed with me. For that I am truly grateful, however, that did not alleviate the fact that I had failed in my role as a husband and as a father. Instead of realizing my dream of being "important" I came to the point where I was totally "impotent".

The day for the bankruptcy hearing arrived. My wife and I were seated to the right of the judge. Arranged in front of us was a whole battery of lawyers representing clients who had claims against me. It was awful. It was degrading. The pressure was intense. The judge would ask questions and I could not answer them. My wife was filling in the blanks and the judge was losing what patience he had. "I am not talking to you," he curtly said to her. Then he turned to me.

"Mister, if you do not start answering these questions, I am going to throw you in jail for contempt."

"Judge, sir, please, this is difficult. Give me ten minutes. Let me have a few minutes to get my head on straight."

"Ten minutes it is. We will take a ten-minute recess; and when we return, you better have the answers to my questions."

Frightened and confused, I made my way across the hall to the men's restroom. Standing all alone in front of the urinal, I cried out, "God, if You are real, I cannot take this any more."

I did not know God. I wasn't even sure if there was a God. I was convinced that there had to be something greater than the creation from which we came. However, I did not know what or whom it might be. I looked at Transcendental Meditation. I looked at the Way International with its practice of strange tongues. I read up on the eastern religions like Buddhism and Hinduism. I visited the Bahia Temple, thinking that universal acceptance of all religions would make things easy. I looked and I listened and still I had an emptiness. It came down to the point where I developed my own philosophy that seemed to answer my questions even though it fell somewhere between weird and wacky. I honestly believed that there was a huge pool of creative energy somewhere out in the cosmos from which everything was created, and when the object's purpose was complete, whether it be a planet or a person, it would return to that pool to be used again.

There was no room for God and yet I stood there in front of that urinal in desperation crying out, "God, if You are real, I cannot take this anymore. If You are out there, please forgive my foolishness."

Suddenly the temperature in that restroom shot up 10 to 15 degrees. It got hot in there. It felt as if lightening had struck me. I was transfixed. I could not move. I felt something reach down through me clear to the soles of my feet. It was incredible. It is impossible to do justice in explaining what happened. All I know is that I could feel all of the filth, and lies and cheating, and partying, and manipulation, the alcoholism, and foul language, the jealousy, the pride, the arrogance, and all those sins that had kept me in bondage being pulled right out of me. I could feel all the garbage I had accumulated over the years moving up through my body, and, as it moved, the hair stood on end. When it came to the top of my head I heard what sounded like a "pop", and it felt as if I was floating, and yet my feet were on solid ground. I turned around in absolute bewilderment and to my amazement, the Lord Jesus Christ walked into that room. Am I going to tell you that I saw Him physically? I do not know if I did or not. All I do know is there was no mistaking who He was. It was not Buddha. It was not Mohammed. It was not Vishnu or one of the Hindu gods. It was not Dr. Moon or the Maharishi or a committee of the above. It was Jesus, and for the first time in my life I understood what it meant to be free. Free from the shackles and chains that come with living your life by yourself for yourself.

You may not be able to relate to or understand what I experienced, however, I know you can relate to the shackles and chains. A young person today would say. "It was totally awesome, dude!"

When I left that restroom and returned to the courtroom, every question was answered to the judge's satisfaction. In the end, after everything was sold and all the expenses were paid, no one lost anything except me. I lost several hundred thousand dollars, but believe me, I received far more than I could ever have lost. In everything that happened I realized one very profound truth. God has a sense of humor. You see, that day was April 1st, 1974. It is true that I lost a great deal; however, I found a relationship with a living, loving, forgiving Savior who willingly entered into a relationship with one of the greatest fools who ever lived.

It would be great if I could tell you that everything turned out fine and everyone lived happily ever after, but I can't. I did not have a clue what to do next. I never had any good teaching on what it meant to be a Christian. I did not have an understanding of the Bible. All I had was a fanatical desire to see my family receive the same thing that I had. I put my wife through ten years of living hell when I was doing my own thing and yet she stayed with me. However, the "new me" frightened her, and my insistence on her receiving the same experience I had began to drive a wedge between us and force her away from me. Could it be that I had found a relationship with God only to sacrifice a relationship with my family?

Surely not! It was a critical time, however, never fear because God was near.

I had a position in the skilled trades with a premier manufacturing company. It was a good job and I enjoyed it very much. I had my own work area and was busy about my business when I heard my name. I turned around thinking it was the gentleman who worked behind me, but there was no one there. Okay, I was mistaken. A few minutes later I once again heard my name just as clear as a bell. I turned around and again there was no one there. Matter of fact, there wasn't anyone in the area. I went out in the aisle and looked. I went over by the machines and looked. There was no one there. Strange, wasn't it? I returned to my work area and once again heard my name. This time the hairs on the back of my neck stood on end.

"Could that be You, God?" I asked.

"Yes, it could be," came the reply

How many would guess that got my attention. We had a conversation that afternoon just like I would be talking to you.

"Do you want to lose your wife?"

Being the articulate person I was, I said, "What?"

"You heard Me, do you want to lose your wife?"

"That's an easy one God – no!"

"Then leave her alone and let Me take care of her. Okay?"

I could not wait to get home and talk to my wife. Not to tell her what happened, but to simply ask for forgiveness. I had to tell her how sorry I was for trying to force something on her that she did not understand. I promised her that I would love her just the way she was and would not say any more. Within days she came to the point where she too wanted to know this Jesus and she invited Him into her life. That's when things started getting interesting. I thought I loved her before, but now it was different. I not only loved her, I was consumed with her and it has not stopped. Thirty-four years later and it is still awesome.

Okay! The time has arrived. Now it is time for **"the rest of the story."**

So sit back, relax, and fill up your coffee cup (it might be easier if you fill it before you sit back) and join me as I share with you the incredible impact that our God has had on the lives of my family, and let me introduce you to several wonderful people who have also experienced the benefits and the blessings of a relationship with the Lord Jesus Christ. They are everyday people just like you and me. People who have come to the understanding and an incredible appreciation of the fact that . . .

God loves the common person!

Today Was Going to be the Day

Yes, sir! Today was going to be the day. There will be no more teasing and no more bullying me around. Today was going to be the day I was going to make it to the diving platform. Pretty strong, daring, and somewhat stupid words from an eight-year-old who could not swim a lick. Just outside of the small northern Indiana town of Shipshewana there is a small lake cleverly named Lake Shipshewana. My aunt and uncle happened to own a small resort on the lake called Beatty's Beach. It was a neat place with three cabins and a quonset hut along with a main lodge that served great chocolate malts. On the shore was a huge circular swing with eight seats. The faster you pushed, the higher the swings would go. There was also a humongous toboggan that seemed to reach to the sky. Well, when you are eight and standing next to it, it seemed like it reached to the sky.

The highlight of our summer was the yearly family pilgrimage to visit Aunt Marcine and Uncle Frank. It was awesome and the closer we got, the more dejected I became because I knew that I was going to be ridiculed and bullied because I could not make it to the diving platform where the big kids hung out. Today, however, was going to be different. I was bound and determined that I was going to make it to the platform. It was very early in the morning. The sun was just coming up when I sneaked out of bed without waking my brother and somehow made it down the stairs. I was surprised the squeaking of the treads did not wake Mom. I made it outside and stood on the beach looking out toward my objective. Yes, sir, today was going to be my big day. I waded out into the water until it was knee high and paused wondering if this was a good idea. I can do it. I am going to do it. I continued to wade out until the water was chest deep. I don't know about this. It sure looked a long way away still. I took another couple of steps and the water was up to my chin. All of a sudden I felt fear and thought this is not going to work. As I turned to return to shallower water, I slipped off into the deep water.

Hey! My feet were not touching the bottom. What happened to the bottom? I tried to scream for help and I could not. I would swallow a mouth full of water each time I tried. I desperately beat the water with my arms trying my best to get closer to the shore. Help me! Somebody please help me. I could not stay on top of the water. I began to sink.

I do not know how long I struggled. I do know there came a time when the struggling stopped and I simply floated in the water. I was totally aware of what was happening around me, however, I could do nothing about it. There was no fear. I was totally relaxed. Suddenly there was a violent movement over me as if a sled from the toboggan had passed right over my head. I began to slowly turn somersaults in the water.

Now don't leave me. Hang in there because this is where things get rather strange. The next thing I remember I am standing on the beach next to this very tall woman. Now remember I was only eight years old yet I can still recall what she looked like as if it was yesterday. She was very tall and pretty. She had long hair pulled back into a bun. She had on a white blouse and a long gray skirt. She was wearing a pair of black high top shoes. I can still remember her gentle blue eyes, and her soft voice as she bent down toward me and called me by name. I had never seen her before. How did she know who I was? "Terry," she said. "You are going to have to be learn to be more careful. There are things you have to do." The next thing I know she was gone. I did not have a clue how she got onto the beach or where she went. The gate was still locked and I was the only one up. I know I was in that water. I know I went too far and stepped into the deep water. I know now that I drowned that morning. I should have been dead and yet I was standing alone on the beach. Who was she? Where did she go? All I could do was sneak back up to bed and ponder tough questions for a confused eight year old. That was until I heard my dad say, "Come on, boys, it is time to go fishing."

I did not learn how to swim until a year later. I guess my uncle got tired of me complaining about the "big guys" picking on me because I could not make it to the diving platform. "Come on, Terry. Let's go for a boat ride," he said one day. Yeah! I loved to go in his boat, however, this time was different. We made it to the middle of the lake where he very gently and very deliberately threw me overboard. "Okay, runt, now swim," he laughingly said. He had a special gift for words. Needless to say I learned to swim that day. Well you might say I learned to do the dog paddle that day. At least I stayed on the surface and made it back to the boat.

Okay, now advance the clock thirteen years because "today was going to be the day". Today was going to be the day my family and I were going to leave on that long awaited vacation. We were going camping with some friends near a small lake in southwest Wisconsin called Yellowstone Lake. We had packed the car the day before because I worked as a chemist in a steel foundry on the night shift, and we were going to leave as soon as I finished work. The drive up was easy and uneventful. My buddy and his wife had already set up their tent by the time we arrived so they helped us with ours. The wives were getting ready to prepare dinner when my buddy said he wanted to take the boat out on the lake. I am not sure you can call it a boat. It was more like a 12-foot dinghy that had to be rowed, however, it served its purpose. We did not notice that a storm was brewing as we made our way across the bay. Suddenly, without warning, the winds began to howl, the rain began to come down in sheets, and the waves became ferocious.

We did what every red blooded fisherman would do under those circumstances. We panicked. It took everything we had to keep the boat moving toward shore. The rain was blowing sideways, the noise was incredible, and, to our dismay, we were being blown directly toward the spillway. On the shore I could barely make out the figure of my wife. She was desperately waving her arms and jumping up and down. Somehow we made it to shore less than a hundred yards from going over the dam. Boats were going down everywhere. We did not realize it until later that two tornadoes had struck near the lake. One touched down on each side and we were caught right in the middle.

Unfortunately, when we made it back to camp, we saw that everything was blown down. None of the tents were still standing. When we took inventory it became obvious that we had a problem. I had one dry pair of underwear, my wife had one dry change of clothes, and my one-year-old son had just a couple of dry diapers. We had no choice but to pack everything back into the car and head home.

Now realize by now I had been up for over twenty-four hours, however, there was nothing else I could do but head home. We crossed the Mississippi River at Dubuque, Iowa, and headed south toward the Quad Cities. I have no idea how long we had been on the road or how far we had driven. All I know is that I woke up just in time to see us heading for a huge triple level sign indicating a double 90-degree turn ahead. Okay. I can handle that, I thought, until I glanced down at the speedometer and saw that it was pegged at 117 miles per hour. Needless to say utter fear gripped me as I realized there was no way I could slow down enough to make it around those 90-degree curves. I did not even have time to cry out to my wife who had fallen asleep herself.

Now hang in there. Do not leave me because this is where it once again gets interesting. I cannot explain it. I certainly do not understand it. All I know is that instantly we were in slow motion. I am not exaggerating one bit. That car did the impossible and made it around a double 90 turn going 117 miles per hour. My wife and my son never even woke up. Needless to say, I freaked out and I had no problem staying awake the rest of the way home. Those things do not happen, or do they?

Okay, now advance the clock another nine years because "today was going to be the day." Today was going to be the day I came to understand what had taken place so many years before. The day began just like any other Saturday. There was nothing special happening, and we had nowhere to go. I had just gone through the bankruptcy. Things were beginning to come together once again. My wife had made her decision to accept Christ Jesus as her Savior. We both were excited about the changes in our lives. Things were good. I had just finished my morning coffee and was ready to settle down with my Bible. I had such a hunger to know more about Jesus. It was hard at times for me to set the Word of God aside long enough to do the things around the house that I needed to do. I opened the Bible to the book of Hebrews and began to read how the Son of God is so much better than the angels. I came to the last verse in chapter one and instantly my eyes became transfixed on what I saw. Surely my lower jaw had to be resting on my lap. From the page leapt these amazing words. "Are not all angels ministering spirits sent to serve those who will inherit salvation?" All of a sudden I was eight years old again and standing next to a tall, beautiful angel hearing her say I needed to learn to be more careful because there were things I needed to do. All of a sudden I was twenty-one years old again in a speeding car cradled in the hands of an angel helping me navigate a double 90 at 117 miles per hour. Those two events were not simply quirks of nature like I had assumed they were. It was the hand of God directing His angels to help me in my moments of greatest need. What happened next surprised even me for I had never found myself lying on my face in the middle of the floor weeping uncontrollably before. I mean, get serious. Grown men do not cry at least until they come face-to-face with an awesome, loving, faithful God.

As miraculous as these two events were, they were BC (before Christ). I did not know God. I did not have a clue that there was a God, and I was not very interested in knowing Him whoever He was. I was content even though I was on my way to a Christless eternity in hell. The truly amazing thing to me is that, even in my ignorance and darkness, He still knew me. He still needed me. He still cared enough to reach down and save my life, not once but twice. Hear what the Word of God says.

> "For You created my inmost being; you knit me together in my mother's womb. I praise you because I am wonderfully made; Your works are wonderful, I know

that full well. My frame was not hidden from You when I was made in the secret place. When I was woven together in the depths of the earth, Your eyes saw my unformed body. All the days ordained for me were written in Your book before one of them came to be." Psalm 139:13-16

I am no more important in God's eyes than you are. The privileges I have found in Christ Jesus are there for you also. Whether you are living in your BC or you know Jesus as your Savior is totally irrelevant. If you take the time and are honest with yourself, you can look back in your life and recall a time when you were amazed and wondered what happened that brought you through some trial or hazardous event. Wow! Where did that come from? How did I make it through that situation? Man, that was a close call. I could have been killed or at least I should have been seriously hurt.

Hello, is there anyone out there? It is time to wake up! You are asleep at the wheel of your life going 117 miles an hour toward ultimate destruction. It is time that you realize there are no coincidences. There is no such thing as luck. You have a loving, caring, awesome God that knows who you are, knows where you are, knows what you are going through, and, in spite of it all, loves you enough to send His angels to work on your behalf. Let's face it. Today is the day that you should begin to realize that there is a very real, very loving, and very caring God that has ordained the number of your days. He is working in your life while waiting patiently for you to come to the point where you realize that you need Him. Joshua, the great leader who led the nation of Israel into the promised land challenged the Israelites in Joshua 24:14,15.

> "Now fear the Lord and serve Him with all faithfulness. Throw away the gods your forefathers worshipped beyond the River and in Egypt, and serve the Lord. But if serving the Lord seems undesirable to you , then choose for yourselves **this day** whom you will serve, whether the gods your forefathers served beyond the River, or the gods of the Amorites, in whose land you are living. But as for me and my household, we will serve the Lord.

We came to know a young couple very well. They were just ordinary people like my wife and I. There was nothing about them that would cause them to stand out in a crowd. They were simply hard working people who loved to spend time together, who enjoyed the pleasures of parenting, and who enjoyed the opportunity to help others. Does that sound a lot like you? Bud, Sharon, and their children lived in a small community not far from us and attended the same church we joined. This particular evening they were returning home from a short trip. It was late. They were not far from home. They had taken the back roads because there was less traffic and they had to get the baby-sitter home. The road was a good blacktop even though it was narrow. As they approached a one-lane bridge, to their surprise and horror, they suddenly noticed a car coming directly toward them at a very high rate of speed. They had nowhere to go. There were metal guardrails on each side of the road to keep the vehicle from falling off into the deep ditch on either side. Surely that guy knew they were there. Why was he not slowing down? This is not good! Sharon screamed as she slid down on the floor in front of her seat. All Buddy could do was shout in a very loud voice: "Jesus", and he also ducked down below the dash anticipating a horrible crash. Nothing happened. A few seconds, which seemed like an eternity, passed and still nothing happened. Bud lifted his head above the steering wheel. The road in front of them was clear. There was no one there. He sat up and glanced in the rearview mirror; and to his surprise he saw that same car flying down the road moving away from them. How? There was not enough room on the bridge for both cars. A couple of days later when they were telling us about what happened, he said: "I should have stayed up. It would have been interesting to see how the Lord delivered us."

My wife and I have had the awesome privilege of knowing many wonderful people who have experienced and recognized the amazing grace of our Lord Jesus Christ, and I would like to take a few minutes and introduce several of them to you. Realize that there are countless testimonies just like Bud and Sharon's or just like Linda's and mine. Testimonies of common people just like you and me who have come to that point in their lives where they truly know that . . .

God loves the common person!

To Have the Faith of a Child

If you had known Sir Charles of Highwood and you were a normal, somewhat intelligent, and mature adult, you would have to agree that he was a messed up mutt. There are dogs who do justice to their breed, however, Sir Charles was not one of them. We definitely had a clash of personalities. He was crazy and yet you better not say that around the boys. They loved that dog and would have been all over your case if you had badmouthed him.

It all began when I, in a moment of weakness, caved into their begging and agreed to let them have a puppy. Puppies are great; unfortunately, they have to grow up. Regardless of what I thought of Sir Charles, he was the toast of the neighborhood. Everyone loved him. I guess I associated that with the fact that everyone did not have to live with him.

I am not sure what you would call him. He was some sort of English breed that resembled a springer except he had long fuzzy white fur with large black spots. As a puppy he was fun to be around, but as he grew he developed a very annoying habit. At night he would sleep on his bed in the garage. It was a large comfortable area and he did not seem to mind. However, every morning when I went to let him out, there would be seven piles of do. Not six or eight.

There would be seven, and they would always be in the same spots on the floor. Come on now, he was outside all day. He could have fertilized the yard. My garage floor did not need it. How disgusting. I tried everything to break him of the habit, however, nothing worked. It finally came to the point where he was no longer welcomed in the house. Charlie was going to go outside one way or the other. I built him a very nice doghouse. It was large. It was comfortable, and with the straw it was warm in the winter.

Watching him was comical. He would walk into the doghouse, turn around three times, move the straw into a precise pattern, and then lie down with his paws draped over the entrance and his muzzle resting on his paws. There he would lie watching the world go by. I must admit that I am not an expert on dog behavior, however, every dog I ever saw had an affinity for rabbits and squirrels with the exception of Sir Charles. I am not sure if he was so comfortable that he did not want to move, or he was so lazy he just did not care, but he would lie there watching a rabbit enjoy a bean salad at the expense of my garden and do nothing about it. Even worse, a pesky squirrel would very boldly walk up to his food dish and feast on the dog food as the dog laid there and watched some three feet away.

Well anyway, the bottom line was the children loved that crazy mutt. As the years went by, and the dog began feeling his age, a gray film began to develop on his eyes. It eventually came to the point where Sir Charles went totally blind. The vet told me that there was not much he could do. What made things difficult was the fact that my wife would do a major cleaning every month and she would never leave the furniture in the same place. Needless to say Sir Charles had a difficult time navigating. Powwow time, boys. Come on, gather around. We need to talk about what we are going to do with Charlie. It was my opinion the only honorable and decent thing to do was to take Charlie to the vet and have him put to sleep. You know, he was getting old and he could not see. How many know that was the wrong thing to say to three boys who loved their dog?

"We can't do that, Dad," they said through a torrent of tears. "Why can't we pray for him?"

"Now wait a minute guys, he is just a dog!"

"But Dad, didn't you tell us that we could ask Jesus for anything and He would do it if we believed?"

"Well, yes, I did because that is what the Bible says, however, Charlie is a dog."

"I know, Dad, but I believe that Jesus can help Charlie," my oldest son replied.

How could I argue with him? "Okay, you boys gather around Charlie and pray for him." My biggest concern was not whether the dog would be healed, but what was I going to tell the boys when nothing happened. Common sense would tell you that Charlie was just a dog. The boys gathered around their beloved pet, laid hands on him, and in their simplistic way asked Jesus to "help Charlie, Lord, please." To my absolute amazement, the scales fell off, the dog began to bark and run around the living room, jump on the boys, and lavishly kiss their faces only as a dog could. He could see!! Sir Charles was totally healed - not only to my amazement, but the vet's amazement also.

Oh, to have the faith of a child. I thought I had a handle on reality and the things of God. However, my three sons brought me to my knees that afternoon and made me realize that there was still a whole lot that I had to learn about an amazing and awesome God. The Word of God in Mark 10:13-16 took on a whole new perspective.

> "People were bringing little children to Jesus to have Him touch them, but the disciples rebuked them. When Jesus saw this, He was indignant. He said to them. 'Let the little children come to Me, and do not hinder them, for the Kingdom of

God belongs to such as these. I tell you the truth, anyone who will not receive the Kingdom of God like a little child will never enter it.' And He took the children in His arms, put His hands on them and blessed them."

I wonder how many of us need to come to the point where we admit that maybe we need to lay down our pride, our prejudices, and our preconceived liturgically canned theologies, and simply begin to trust Jesus and what His Word says.

It was around this same time that we received word from our pediatrician that there was a problem with our second son. We had known for sometime that he had a curved spine. It was a condition that he was born with, however, we did not realize how serious it was until he reached eight years old. The doctor told us that we needed to be very careful with him. He would always be handicapped to the point where he would never be able to play baseball, football, or any other contact sport. That was a devastating revelation to an eight-year-old who wanted to be involved with the rest of the kids in the neighborhood.

"Daddy, I want to run and play with the other guys. Isn't there something that can be done for my back?" he asked me one afternoon while resting on my lap. Without giving me a chance to answer, he continued, "Jesus healed Charlie's eyes, surely He can make my back strong, can't He?"

What is a father going to say? "Do you think He can, son?"

"Yes, I do, Daddy."

Powwow time again. The whole family gathered around Scott and began to ask Jesus to heal him just like He did Charlie. For a normal person, when they stand straight and stretch their arms out in front of them, the fingertips will touch each other. Their arms will be the same length. When someone has a curved spine and he tries it, there will be a difference in length. The more severe the curvature, the greater the difference. When my son tried it, there was a difference of almost an inch, which is huge. As the children, my wife and I began to seek help from Jesus, we watched as his spine straightened out right before our eyes, and we saw his arms adjust to the point where his fingertips touched each other. Scott was totally healed. The doctor was astonished as he verified the fact that something miraculous had happened and his spine was no longer curved but absolutely normal. My son went on to play linebacker and lineman for the high school football team. I pitied the poor running back who got in his way. He also went on to play legion baseball where he excelled at second base and catcher. Today he is in his early forties and an awesome specimen of a man. He tips the scales at 260 and none of it is fat. He is very strong and very active. Why? Because our God cannot help but respond to child-like faith.

Early in my ministry, I had the privilege of conducting a campground ministry. There was a large campground not far from where we lived. Every Sunday afternoon during the summer a young couple would go with me and we would hold a service for the campers. The operators of the campground let us use an old tractor and hay wagon to go around the grounds and pick up those who wanted to come. The services were held under a picnic pavilion. There were times when 75 people came to enjoy the afternoon with us.

I can remember one particular day very well. It was bright and warm. A nice breeze rustled through the leaves and the grass. It was a great day. The young couple with me had just finished leading the people in several popular worship songs and I was getting ready to share a simple message with those gathered around when a child next to me let out a yell and began to cry loudly. He had leaned over and, in doing so, put his hand right on a bee that naturally resented the intrusion and stung him in the palm of his hand. It was obvious very quickly that he was allergic to bee stings because his hand became very red and puffy. His parents were freaking out when I took him in my arms and placed him on my lap. I asked him if he believed Jesus could take care of his hand and with tears streaming down his face, he said "yes". We began to pray and ask Jesus to respond to his child-like faith and heal his hand. I am convinced of one thing; those who were there that afternoon had never witnessed the power and grace of a miracle-working, loving God responding to the faith of a child. They were amazed as they witnessed the pain leave and the swelling subside right before their eyes. Jesus completely restored his hand as if nothing had ever happened. Needless to say, "we had church that afternoon."

It absolutely amazes me to hear people scoff and ridicule the things of God without giving Him a chance. Having questions and maybe even some doubts are natural responses when the miraculous happens. These events I am sharing took place in the lives of children. They were children who had not come to the place where preconceived ideas, theologies, or outright false teachings had hindered or stymied their faith. Their faith was simple. Their faith was pure. Their faith was uncluttered and honest. That is the type of faith that Jesus referred to in Mark. That is the type of faith He expects all of us to have. That is the type of faith that He always responds to.

There was a young man who entered my life many years ago. He was a very troubled young man who was desperately seeking an identity and an answer to who he was. It was difficult for him to recognize any value in himself. He came from a broken home, and no matter how hard he tried, he could not win the approval of his mom or dad.

For several years I helped our local Boys Club, and every year we would take a group of eight- and nine-year-olds to a baseball game in St. Louis. Our little town was located exactly halfway between Chicago and St. Louis, and heated rivalries between Cub fans and Cardinal fans were in evidence everywhere. This particular year we were to take them to a doubleheader between the Cardinals and the Philadelphia Phillies in St. Louis.

Now the young man I was referring to was 13 years old, which made him too old to qualify for the trip; however, the club leadership thought that it would be great therapy if he went. In order to not make the other boys his age angry or disappointed, he was appointed co-chaperone and assigned to my car. So off we went. Eight boys eight-and nine-years-old, a thirteen-year-old co-chaperone, and myself left for

St. Louis. I am glad I had a station wagon because it provided just enough room for everyone.

The games were long. It probably would have been sufficient to sit through one game; however, there were two and the boys wanted to stay. During the second game the weather turned sour and it began to rain. After sitting through a rain delay the decision was made to pull the plug and return home before the weather got too severe. It was not long before the eight young boys in the back fell asleep. The co-chaperone sat staring out of the window. He had been sullen and quiet all evening. He said very little, if anything, all the way down, through the game, or as we started home. He simply sat there and watched the storm pick up in intensity. I must say, I have seldom, if ever, seen lightning and heard thunder like I did that evening. The lightning lit up the car like it was the middle of the afternoon, and the thunder literally shook the car. The winds howled. The rain blew across the highway in sheets. I have no idea why I did not stop and wait out the storm. I do not take chances with my own kids let alone someone else's, and yet we continued across central Illinois on Interstate 55. It was amazing the youngsters in the rear did not wake up. About an hour from home the young man turned to me and somewhat caught me by surprise when he asked me, "Do you believe in Jesus?" "Why, yes, I do," I replied.

Nothing more was said until fifteen minutes later when he once again turned to me and asked, "Is He real?" "Why do you ask ?" I asked him. He began to open up and tell me about a girl who had befriended him. It was difficult for him to make friends and he had few, however, she really seemed to care. She had told him that he needed to get to know Jesus. Jesus could help him and give him what he was looking for. For the next thirty or forty minutes we had an awesome discussion concerning the love of Christ Jesus and the promises in the Word of God. We talked about what Jesus could do for him if he would only believe and accept Him as his Savior.

In the mean time we had turned west on Highway 21. We were only a few minutes from home and the storm was still raging. The wind was still howling and the rain was still coming down in torrents. Without really thinking about it, I turned to the young man and casually said, "We are going to have to ask the Lord to stop this rain so that we can get these boys home without getting wet." Instantly we drove out of a wall of water. I am not kidding. You could look in the rearview mirror, even though it was late, and see a wall of water behind us. That got the young man's attention and every hair on his neck seemed to stand on end. His eyes were as big as half dollars as he turned to me and said, "Mr. J. if it starts raining again after we get home, you are going to have me scared half to death."

"Whoa there, what have we been talking about for the last hour? Can't you see that Jesus is reaching out to you? He stopped that rain in answer to our request just for you. He loves you and wants you to know that He is real, and He is interested in you, and He wants to come into your life and make a difference." That night a troubled young man met Jesus as his friend and savior.

We made it home and all eight of the boys and the co-chaperone were delivered to their anxious parents without one drop of rain hitting any of them. I pulled into our driveway, got out of the car, and in the few seconds it took to cover the thirty feet to the door, I got drenched.

I would like to say that we became very close friends; however, I cannot because soon afterward the family moved and he walked out of my life. I have not heard from him since. That was over thirty years ago, and yet I am totally convinced that, no matter where he is, he is still solid with the Lord. Jesus, in His love and compassion, reached out to a hurting thirteen-year-old boy and showed Himself to be exactly what that young girl said He would be.

I know that there are those right now who are reading this book who can relate to what that young man was going through. The situations are different, the circumstances are different, and yet there is a tremendous similarity because of the loneliness, the hurting, the frustration, the feeling of insignificance, the rejection, and the uncertainty. These are devastating emotions that literally place the individual in bondage. Understand that thirteen-year-old was no one special. He was just an ordinary kid who needed a relationship with an awesome, loving, and caring Savior just like you do. Jesus can stop the wind and the rain in your life. He can bring peace in the storm, revelation in the darkness, and give value when there seems to be none. The only difference between you, my sons, the young camper, and my co-chaperone is that they came to the point in their lives where they were glad that . . .

God loves the common person!

The Enforcer Falls

If we look back in our lives, I am sure we would all be able to point to one or two unique characters who left a lasting impression on us. A young man named Steve would fill that bill for me. He was definitely unique in his own special way, and most of us would find it difficult, if not impossible, to relate to his story. Difficult in the sense that few of us have ever experienced the kind of events that were a common part of his every day. In reality, however, there is no difference between you, Steve, and myself. The similarity boils down to the fact that he dealt with the same emotions we deal with. He dealt with the same emptiness, loneliness, frustration, bitterness, resentment, and rejection that we do. We are all the same on the inside, it is our circumstances and situations that separate us. In Steve's case his circumstances are so outside of the box there is no way I could do them justice, therefore, he is going to explain what happened in his own words. So sit back, relax, break out the popcorn and soda, and let this amazing young man simply wow you.

My story begins on an evening that was not unlike hundreds of other evenings before it. Nothing special was happening. My father was working in the garage on his bike. Several friends and I were lounging around with a few beers when suddenly everything changed. The silence was shattered by the staccato of blazing guns and the sound of lead hitting the walls. The whole world seemed to have gone mad. Without hesitation I grabbed a revolver I kept on the table next to my chair and ran out the back door just in time to see a car pulling away. With the precision of an expert marksman, I emptied a clip of 38 caliber slugs into the vehicle. I could see the figures of four people trying to take cover. The rear window disintegrated as the car accelerated away from the curb. How they managed to elude the return fire is beyond me.

As I turned toward my buddies who were also shooting at the car, I noticed the figure of my father lying in a pool of blood not far from the entrance to the garage. He had been shot in the head and had also received a blast from a shotgun in the back. The bullet had entered near the ear and traveled down the neck where it lodged between his ear and his shoulder. It was amazing that he was still alive. My buddies quickly called the authorities and requested an ambulance. By the time they arrived my father was standing and we had pretty much stopped the bleeding. Knowing my father the way I did, it should not have surprised me when he refused medical help, however, it did. He was carrying enough lead in his body to kill him from lead poisoning, and yet he would not let them help him. For hours after the incident I worked to clean the wounds and dig the pellets from his back. The slug that hit him in the head entered just in front of the ear and lodged in his neck. Every night for weeks I watched him as he forced the slug back up the entry path. He would push and pull until the pain became so intense he would almost pass out. An inch a night, night after night he would manipulate the slug until he finally had it at the point of entry. Unfortunately, by the time he got it that far, the entry point had completely healed over. With a great amount of fortitude and effort he literally forced the slug out of his head through his ear. Don't ask me how. I don't know. He just did.

The local officials and the FBI paid us several visits after that and informed us that a rival gang had reportedly buried two bodies along a stretch of abandoned railroad tracks. They were not sure of the exact location, however, they had several leads, and one of them indicated that we might have information on what happened. There was another young man in critical condition in the local hospital with a hole in his head. It appeared that we were treading on thin ice and possibly facing some serious prison time. As sticky as the situation was, I was not too overly concerned. After all, that possibility came with the territory and the style of life I was leading. I know that one of those guys buried along the track could just as easily have been me. I was living in a jungle where only the fittest and the quickest survived.

My story actually began several years earlier in the family garage where my brother, a few friends, and I laid the foundation for a motorcycle club called the Grim Reapers. In the five years the gang operated, it became one of the largest and most powerful in the Midwest with large chapters in Illinois, Iowa, and Minnesota. My brother became national president and I was appointed one of the national enforcers. The Grim Reapers' name, at one time or another, appeared in many of the large national newspapers. Articles appeared in several large magazines, and several television shows had spots highlighting our activities. Needless to say, the articles and the spots were not too flattering. The more notoriety we received, the larger we became. As we added members, the more pressure we felt from rival gangs who accused us of stepping into their territory. Rumbles and riots between clubs began to occur regardless of where we went. As tempers grew shorter and fights became more frequent, the methods used became more deadly. The tools of our warfare evolved from fists to clubs, then from clubs to chains and knives, and from knives to guns. Eventually it came to the point where anything went regardless of the consequences.

My brother and I were sitting at the breakfast table one morning enjoying a fresh cup of coffee and going over some plans for an upcoming event when suddenly the predawn stillness was shattered by a tremendous blast followed a few seconds later by another one. Dazed, we grabbed our guns and ran down the apartment stairs. I was not prepared for what we saw. The garage with my father's living quarters above it was demolished. The whole front of the building had simply disappeared and smoke billowed out of what was left. The devastation from the blast was everywhere. I could not help but think there was no way my father could have lived through that. All I remember was looking around for someone to take out. It did not matter who it might be. If someone had been standing in the street at that time, I would have taken them down not caring if they were responsible or not. I hurt inside at the thought of losing my dad, and it was all I could do to find a phone to notify the authorities. When I returned to the chaos, I was amazed at the sight of my father standing by what was left of the garage with my brother supporting him with one arm and holding his rifle in the other. It was impossible, and yet he lived through both explosions with just an injured toe. The excitement of seeing him alive, however, soon turned to anger and frustration, and I swore that those responsible would pay dearly for what happened.

Hour after hour and day after day I worked at perfecting and fine tuning my skills in the martial arts. I became proficient at judo, karate, boxing, street wrestling, and marksmanship. I became more than a simple enforcer. I became a deadly machine. I was totally nasty. I would beat to a pulp anyone who thought he was tougher than me. My reputation spread and I became greatly feared. My days were spent working out in my gym, and my evenings were spent in the taverns around town. I have fought with the best. I have drunk with the meanest. I have seen incredible fights where people ended up shot and stabbed or had bottles broken over their heads. I have walked the streets with men so burned out on drugs they looked like death warmed over.

My world consisted of a series of smoke-filled bars where half-naked women bumped and ground to the sound of the go-go bands I played in. It was a world of fornication, impurity, drunkenness, adultery, and mistrust where men spent grocery money on gambling, booze, and loose women instead of food for their families. It was a world where married men made fools of themselves over married women who were looking for a quick trick. I lived in a world where the darkness of night was never penetrated by the light of day.

Altercations with the law became a daily exercise in futility until two local officers were found beaten within an inch of their lives. Assuming we were the ones who caused the injuries, warrants were immediately issued for the arrest of my brother, several friends, and myself. We were assumed guilty and indiscriminately beaten about our heads and backs. I saw my brother take several severe blows to his head which contained a steel plate as a result of injuries he suffered in 'Nam. Anger swelled up inside of me and I screamed and threatened the officers only to be taken down and once again kicked and beaten. Battered and bruised, I was thrown into a cell with my hands still cuffed behind me. For hours I had to suffer excruciating pain from the beatings and the mace that had been sprayed into my face and eyes. The ensuing weeks became a nightmare as the courts made a shambles out of the justice system. No one wanted to listen to our version of what happened. It seemed as if a verdict had been reached even before the trial began. Our requests for polygraph tests and our demands that the officers involved also take the tests were completely ignored. During the proceedings an officer actually perjured himself and the defense refused to react. It seemed like there was a conspiracy against us. After wasting $10,000 on legal fees, I was fined $500 and placed on two years' probation.

Hatred for the system and authorities who represented it encompassed me like never before.

I could think of nothing else but revenge, and it finally drove the one remaining thing in my life that had value away. My girl friend had come to the point where she had enough and she walked out in frustration. The feelings of loneliness and despair were not new to me, however, I can't ever remember being so empty and alone after she left.

Man, what was I doing to myself? What was I trying to prove? What could I do or where could I go? For the first time in my life I did not have the answers I needed. I look back on those days, and I can see a gradual change beginning that would eventually dramatically alter my entire way of thinking. I did not make any dramatic decision or earthshaking commitment. It was the beginning of a gradual process working in me. It started when a young lady who had crossed my path before came back into my life. Up to that time I had totally ignored her because she did not fit my definition of a tough guy's girl. However, no matter how hard I tried to ignore her, I could not put her out of my mind. Eventually a crazy type of relationship developed. I could not believe that she even wanted to be around me. She came from a different world, she spoke a different language, she enjoyed simple pleasures, and she was definitely not accustomed to the violent, ungodly world I lived in. She would constantly talk about a special friend of hers named

Jesus whom she honestly believed could change my life and make it better. She even had the audacity to ask me to take her to church. I refused to believe what I was hearing. If I ever went into a church, the ceiling would collapse on me. In my entire life I had never once done anything that would allow church people to accept me. It got to the point where there were times I just wanted to run and hide when I saw her coming, and yet there was something that made me stay. Finally, being the clever kind of guy I am, I made a bargain with her. I would take her to church one time and only one time if she absolutely swore that she would never ask me again. Agreed! Deal done.

I could feel a battle raging inside of me as we entered the sanctuary. I had no idea what to expect. For someone who feared no one, I was filled with an unnatural apprehension. People had to notice me. What would they think of my long hair and obvious look of displeasure. I was amazed that no one took offense or seemed too overly concerned. Matter of fact, they were very friendly. It did not seem to matter that my "food" stood for everything they rejected as the devil's food. As my nervousness eased, my attention was drawn to the words of the preacher. He must have known that I was coming. It seemed as if he was deliberately talking at me. He knew exactly where I was coming from and the type of personal hell I had put myself through over the past several years. Hurt, loneliness, frustration, and fear swept over me as visions of my past raced across my mind. When I heard the verdict pronounced for those who sinned, I knew I was in trouble for I had to be numbered among the chief sinners. When I heard the sentence of eternal death and damnation passed on those who were lost in their sins, the fear became even more intense. Why me? Why are you picking on me? I was suffocating as the weight of the realization of my condition crushed down on me. I wanted to run. I wanted to hide. No place to go. What was I doing there? Then I heard that name again. The name the girl I came with used so many times, and so many times I simply rejected. I heard the preacher as he began to tell me a story about a man who gave His life so that I could have forgiveness of all my sins. It was a story of a man who came into this world to serve people and those He came to serve turned their backs on Him and mocked Him and spit in His face. Although He was not guilty of any crime, they found Him worthy of death and they nailed Him to a cross. I heard the story of an innocent man who took the sins of all mankind upon Himself, and in so doing, He guaranteed my forgiveness and salvation. He was crucified and buried and on the third day He rose from the dead. He is alive, and my heart began to burn inside of me as I heard these words, "It does not matter who you are or what you have done. You do not have to be anyone special. Jesus did not come to save the righteous. He came to save the sick. He came to save the lost sinner." The preacher went on to say, "You can be made new. Your life can change and become worthwhile in the eyes of God." I knew that I had to make a decision that night. Was I going to continue in my world of decadence and sin, or was I going to accept that new life free from pain, anxiety, fear, loneliness, and desperation. My whole insides were consumed with emotions foreign to my character. I could even feel tears running down my cheeks. That was new to me. I had not wept in many years.

When the altar call was given and those who knew they were not right with the Lord were encouraged to come forward, I literally ran to the front of the church, and that morning before the entire congregation and God Himself the "mighty enforcer" fell. As I asked Jesus into my life, I felt the burdens of my entire past life lift right off my shoulders. A sense of peace that I cannot describe swept over me. As if scales had fallen from my eyes, I could see people from an entirely new perspective. I could love them instead of hating them, and that is an attitude that grows stronger and stronger every day I am with Jesus. I absolutely knew that I was a new creation in Christ and my life would never be the same.

For years I allowed satan to control my whole existence. I lived like a hermit and I had little or no respect or trust for others. There were times when I felt so lonely and depressed that I actually considered ending it all because there was nothing worth going on for. Satan almost won the victory in my life, but thanks to a living, loving, caring Savior who sent a young girl into my life, I now walk in victory with Jesus. Those desires of the flesh that held me in bondage and had me on a spiral course leading straight to hell have been replaced by a hatred for sin. The music I once played night after night for satan I now play for the Lord. The temper and the grudges that controlled my thinking have been replaced with a sincere attitude of forgiveness. I can forgive those who persecuted me and sought my life. I can even pray for them that they also would come to know Jesus as I have.

A few of my friends and part of my family have given their hearts to Jesus; however, most of my family and many of my old friends have rejected me. They have very little to do with me anymore, however, God has replaced them with new Christian friends who are always there when temptations call. I consider the greatest miracle in my life to be the saving grace of Jesus making me into a new person. His love has not stopped there, however. I was a hopeless diabetic and I also suffered from epilepsy. I came down with diabetes as a young person, and my daily routine has been dictated by strict diets and thousands of insulin shots due to a pancreas that refused to function. Since I met Jesus as my savior, however, I have seen promises in the Word of God that have changed my life dramatically. I saw that we were promised health and healing. I had the elders of the church anoint me with oil and pray for me according to the fifth chapter of James. We agreed that Jesus was going to touch my body and put it back together again. The same Jesus who cleansed the lepers, healed the sick, gave sight to the blind, made the lame to walk, and even raised the dead touched me. I heard a voice inside of me tell me that I was going to be totally healed. The last time I went to the doctors, they were amazed and had to give me a series of tests. They do not understand it. They do not know how it happened, but my pancreas is beginning to function and produce insulin. They told me it had to be a miracle because those things do not just happen. I got news for those doctors – yes they do! They happen when you serve a miracle-working God. Since that visit my dependence on foreign sources of insulin has greatly diminished, and there will come a day when I am no longer going to need shots. Praise God! I will be able to eat whatever I want. Well almost anything.

Another awesome miracle is that I have not had another seizure since I accepted Christ as savior. That in itself is huge. Thank you, Jesus!

That pretty young girl who Jesus sent my way is now my wife and we are totally content and happy in serving the Lord together. There isn't enough gold or silver in the world that would tempt me back into that old life. I am so thankful that I have come to know that . . .

God loves the common person!

Did You Listen To Your Son Last Night?

For all practical purposes Dave, his wife, and their children have to be considered an "all-American" family. They are successful, content, and solid in their relationships with Jesus. Dave is a hard working, blue collar, everyday Joe who has an unusual compassion for those less fortunate. His heart is for those who, for a variety of reasons, find themselves homeless, on the streets, and with nowhere to go. For several years he would take a day a week, no matter what the weather, and join them. It was important to him that those with little knew that someone understood and cared about them, and what they were going through. Eventually he opened a coffeehouse in downtown Peoria, Illinois. It soon became a safe haven for the many have-nots. It was a place where they could come and enjoy a cup of hot cocoa or coffee, get a simple warm meal, and someone to talk to who would not look down his nose at them. His love and concern were responsible for bringing fifty derelicts and indigents to Jesus in one year.

His children have all grown into fine, healthy adults who have all dedicated their lives to serve their Lord. Life is good, and they are very blessed, however, it wasn't always that good or that easy. Matter of fact, there was a time, early in their marriage, when life was very difficult and their relationship was held together by a thin, precarious thread. In order to do justice to the situation, let Dave explain what happened in his own words.

Hi there. My name is Dave, and I am excited to have an opportunity to share with you what has happened in my life. Every time I think about it, I am amazed because He has done so much for me even though I did not deserve it. I am no one special. I am just like so many other guys. I look back and see that my early years were nothing to brag about. I was lucky to even make it into eighth grade in school. I never did learn how to read or write. What I did learn, however, was to fight, drink, and party. I was pretty good at them. About the only real break I got was a job with an aggregate company. I learned how to operate a large crane that unloaded barges carrying sand and gravel. It wasn't much and yet it would have been sufficient to support my family if I hadn't spent so much on booze. I would work hard all day and drink hard all night. Unfortunately, that forced my wife to seek employment just to pay the bills. It soon came to the point where she had enough. She was fed up with working so hard and worrying about who would take care of the children. I wasn't around. I was too busy doing my own thing.

I was sitting on my usual stool in my favorite bar joking around with what I thought were friends.

I guess they would call me a friend as long as I had money to buy the beer. Suddenly my wife walked in. She came up to me and informed me that I was going home with her. I tried to convinced her that she was not going to tell me what I was going to do. That was not the cool thing to do. At the top of her lungs she informed me that I was leaving "NOW!! That was embarrassing. What nerve. She had no business doing that in front of everyone. How was I going to face them the next time. Wait until I get home. I'll tell her a thing or two. So I thought. She stole my thunder when she informed me that she was not going to put up with me any more. She was going to leave me and take the children. I did not know what to think. I closed myself in my bedroom and proceeded to get angry and frustrated. She is just kidding. Where would she go. Who would she stay with. She is not serious. She will come to her senses in the morning. My pity party was interrupted by a knock on the door and the voice of my five-year-old son saying, "Daddy, I need to tell you something."

"Go away. I don't want to talk to you right now."

"But Daddy, I have to tell you something."

"I said get out of here. Go pester your mother."

"Please Daddy?"

"Okay, but make it quick."

He slowly opened the door. He did not know what to expect. He came to the front of the bed and looked right at me, and in a clear, steady voice said, "Daddy, if you do not ask Jesus to forgive you, you will die and go to hell. I don't want you to go away, Daddy."

What kind of garbage was that? Now I was really getting angry. "Get out of here and leave me alone," I yelled, and he left. The next thing I knew the alarm was going off and it was time to get up for work. Another day, another splitting headache, and a lot of unanswered questions greeted me. I guess I would have to wait to straighten out my wife. The day started out just like any other day. Barges waiting at the dock. Gravel to be unloaded. It really got to be a boring routine. There were times I wanted to quit and find something better, however, not having an education stopped me. So there I was doing the same-o same-o. I definitely was not prepared for what happened next.

One of my more serious hang-ups, other than booze, was the fact that I was extremely prejudiced and I really did not know why. Maybe it was because my father hated people of color. There happened to be a big black man named Jim working with me. I had very little to do with him and very seldom started a conversation with him. You might say I just tolerated him. I was busy doing my job when I noticed him standing next to the machine.

"What do you want?"

"I need to ask you a question."

"Can't you see that I am busy?"

"Please, Dave, I know how you feel about me, however, it is important."

"If it concerns the job I am doing, let the boss tell me."

"Dave, it is not like that. I need to ask you a very important question."

"Okay, get it over with."

"Dave, did you listen to your son last night? What he said to you is true."

Needless to say, I was not prepared for what he said, and it definitely got my attention. What is going on here? Is there a conspiracy with my wife and Jim against me? No! That is impossible. This is insane. There is no way he could know what happened in my bedroom the night before. What is going on? The rest of the workday was a real challenge. I was totally confused and did not know what to think or say. The longer I thought about what Jim said, the more nervous and agitated I became. Could there be something to this? What if this Jesus guy is who they say He is? Do you really think there is a hell? Why would He send me there? I never killed anyone or stole anything. I may have my problems, but I am an all right kind of guy. By the time the quitting whistle blew, my shirt was wringing wet with sweat. I was very nervous and somewhat frightened. Normally I would stop by the tavern and have a couple of beers before I went home, however, this day was different. I drove straight home. Karen and the kids were nowhere around. I went straight into my bedroom where I thought I would feel safe and things would settle down, but that was not the case. The fear and the apprehension just grew more severe until I thought I was going to explode. I ran into my closet and shut myself in. What is going on? Am I losing my mind?

In the quietness of the darkness I could think of nothing else to do but take a chance. I did not know what to expect. I was not sure what to think or say.

All I know is that I cried out, "Jesus, I do not know if You are real or not. If You are, I do not want to die, and I sure do not want to go to hell, if there is such a place. I guess I want You to forgive me like my son said." You talk about being speechless. There is no way I can even begin to describe what happened next. It seemed as if a huge light was turned on inside of me and I saw for the first time all the rottenness, lies, abuse, swearing, drinking, and lust that were destroying me. They were being pulled right out of me. All the hatred and distrust just seemed to vanish. I no longer felt a desire for alcohol. I did not feel the need to use foul language to make a point anymore. Matter of fact, I have not had a drink or used profanity since that day. All I know is that Jesus walked into that closet and introduced Himself to me. I did not actually see Him or hear Him, but I knew that He was the one who made the changes in my life. There is no way I could have made them on my own. I had a rather vivid imagination; however, I could never have thought up something like that. It had to take someone greater than me to clean me out like He did.

By then Karen and the kids had returned home and things really began to get interesting. My son ran up to me and gave me a hug, and, for the first time in a long time, I grabbed him up in my arms and simply hugged him. He was so surprised he forgot what he was going to tell me. I guess the tears running down my cheeks really caught my wife's attention. "David, what in the world is wrong with you? What has happened? Now what have you done?" Not unrealistic questions considering she had never seen me cry before. I can imagine the shock she must have experienced. "Jesus is real" I cried. "He has forgiven me. I love you," I said as I grabbed her and just held on to her. I do not know what was going through her mind. All she did was stand there with her mouth wide open as I held on and cried on her shoulder. It took several minutes for me to calm down enough to tell her what had happened. Needless to say, she was speechless for some time, and I had never seen her like that. It was great. It was awesome. There was so much I wanted to say to her. I was amazed at how easy it was for me to ask her for forgiveness and to tell her that I loved her. I was amazed at what I saw when I looked at my children. They were mine. They were special. They were beautiful. That day we all began to fall in love with each other, and, best of all, with Jesus.

I could not wait until the next workday. When I got to the yard, I looked around for Jim and saw him by the office. I literally ran up to him and grabbed him and gave him a big hug. "Thank you, thank you, thank you. I do not know how you knew that my son had said anything to me. I guess that is not important. I am just thankful that you came over to me and talked to me," I said to him. He was totally shocked. You might say that my actions literally blew him away. When I calmed down enough to explain to him what happened, we both began to shout and cry. The rest of the crew thought we had gone off the deep end. We were like a couple of kids celebrating. It was great. I look back on that experience now and I am so thankful that I had a man like Jim who I could rely on. He has truly become one of my closest friends. I love and appreciate him because I knew nothing about the Bible or Christianity and he became my mentor. I had only heard stories about Jesus. Instead of spending time in the bars, I now spent hours with Jim asking him all kinds of questions and listening to him as he makes the things of the Bible come alive to me. I would go home at night and tell Karen what Jim had said that day. Every evening I would ask my wife to read the Bible to me. I had such a hunger for the Word of God.

It amazed me how a life that had been a burden became a life of joy, peace, expectation, and excitement. I love life. I love my family. I love my newfound church family and yet there was something missing inside of me. I wanted to know everything there was to know about Jesus. I would lay on my bed and pick up the Bible that sat on the table next to me and I would become so frustrated because it was just black and white to me. It had no meaning because I could not read. I had to wait until someone was around who could and would read it to me. How frustrating. One evening I was resting in my bedroom. It had been a long day and I was sore and tired. I picked up my Bible and held it next to my chest. "Lord God, You know that I love You. You know how thankful I am that you saved me and forgave me, but God, I can't get to know You like I want to because I cannot read. Do you think maybe You could help me?" I really did not know what to expect. I am not sure if I expected anything to happen, however, I slowly opened the Bible and was totally shocked as words began leaping off the pages. Words I recognized and understood. Hey, I can read! I ran out of the room and yelled to my wife, "Karen, I can read. Listen to this." I opened up the Bible to the New Testament and began to read the Gospel of John. Tears began to stream down both of our cheeks. It was amazing. It was exciting. For the first time in my life I could read. I even took the evening paper and began to read what it said.

I am not sure you will ever really understand the significance of that miracle in my life. When you are illiterate, it is like you are blind. The sense of loneliness and insignificance at times can be overwhelming. To be able to read was like being reborn into someone significant. To be able to function on my own without relying on someone else was huge. Jesus not only gave me the ability to read, I could also write. My penmanship lacked something to be desired, however, my name became Dave and not just X. What an exciting time.

Can I tell you how this all happened? No. I do not have a clue. I guess the important thing is not how it happened, but that it did happen and why it happened. It happened because Jesus loved me enough, even though I was sick in my sins, that He refused to give up on me. He used a five-year-old boy and a wonderful black brother to bring me to the point where I was willing to give Him a chance. Is my story unique? The circumstances may be, but the need isn't. I would venture to say that there are many right now who have gone through or are going through much of what I put myself through. If you find yourself in a similar environment as I was, with the lies, the alcohol, the foul language, the arrogance, and the pride, you are probably blaming everyone you can think of except the one who should be blamed, and that is yourself. I made the decisions that caused my life to be what it was just like you are making the decisions that have made your life what it is today. I have news for you that you need to hear. If Jesus would reach down and touch my life, which He did, He will and can do the same for you. I am no one special. I am no different than countless other gals and guys just like you. You can also take a chance with Jesus and ask Him to forgive and change you. Do you know why? Because . . .

God loves the common person!

Hey! I Want to Talk to You

Who in his right mind would honestly believe that a loving, caring, all powerful God would not talk to His people? That is an easy question to answer. A very high percentage of professing Christians believe that God cannot or does not desire to talk to His people. Hogwash! I guess I was one of the lucky ones who heard Him speak before someone told me He couldn't. It does not make sense to me that a God who loves me so much that He would send His only Son to die for me would not communicate with me. Jesus alludes to the fact that the believers are His bride when questioned why His disciples did not fast according to the tradition of the elders.

> "Now John's disciples and the Pharisees were fasting. Some people came and asked Jesus, 'How is it that John's disciples and the disciples of the Pharisees are fasting, but Yours are not?' Jesus answered, 'how can the guests of the bridegroom fast while he is with them. But the time will come when the bridegroom will be taken from them, and on that day they will fast." Mark 2:18,19

Jesus is in a love relationship with the "born again" believers. Why would He not want to communicate with them?

I cannot imagine living with the woman I love and never saying anything to her. What would it be like to come home from a busy day at work, get cleaned up, have a good meal, lounge around for several hours, go to bed, get up in the morning, go to work again, and never say a word to your spouse or never have your spouse say a word to you? How long would the relationship last? Exactly! It would not. A successful marriage is built upon the ability to communicate, therefore, it might not be a bad idea to begin communicating with your Lord.

I guess that is enough meddling. Where were we? You would have liked Grandma Rapp. She was a bona fide character. She was one fantastic woman who loved people and her Lord, however, that wasn't always the case. When she was younger she was a supervisor in the oldest profession on earth. She was the madame of a bordello. In other words, she ran a house of ill repute. No one messed with Grandma Rapp. There came a day, however, when she began to question her life and what she was doing with it. That is a perfect invitation for the Lord to start speaking and speak He did. Needless to say Grandma was shocked when God began to tell her that she was living in a counterfeit world where love had little or no meaning. He offered her a relationship that had substance, a relationship that was more than a one-night stand, and a relationship that would give her life a sense of dignity and purpose that she was so desperately seeking.

"What will it cost me?" she asked Him.

"It will cost you nothing and at the same time it will cost you everything."

"Lord, I do not understand. What are you saying, everything?"

"Simply believe that what I am saying to you is true, ask for forgiveness, invite Me into your life, and trust Me with everything you are."

"But Lord, how do I know I can trust you? I am so used to people taking advantage of me."

"Grandma, just give Me a chance to prove Myself to you. I will not fail you."

Such a deal He had for her. How could she not accept it? Accept it she did and what a transformation. A hard, calculating woman became a marvelous, warm individual who would do anything for her Lord.

She was traveling on Interstate 55 one bright afternoon on her way to St. Louis. As she drove past a quaint little church, the Lord spoke to her and told her He wanted her to stop at the church and give the men inside a check for $119.62.

"But Lord, there is no one there. The parking lot is empty."

"Grandma, I asked you to do something for Me. It is important."

"Lord, I do not understand. There is no one there."

"Grandma!"

"Okay Lord, I will trust You and do what You ask."

She left the interstate at the next exit and turned onto a service road that led her back to the church. As she pulled into the parking lot, she was amazed to see two men, the pastor and his elder, come out of the side door. They had parked their cars behind the building where Grandma could not see them. She walked up to them and said, "I do not expect you to understand, however, the Lord told me to stop and give you this", and she handed them the check for $119.62. To her surprise, they took one look at it and both began to rejoice and cry. With tears streaming down his face, the pastor revealed how the church was facing difficulties and they had a heating bill they could not pay. The two men had just asked the Lord for help. They said, "Lord, if you really want this church to stay open, we need help. Would you please send someone to help us with this heating bill as a sign that You do care and You still want us to minister in this area?" You got it. The heating bill was for $119.62. Coincidence? Not a chance. The Lord communicates with His people. He communicated with Grandma Rapp in a recognizable voice, and He communicated to the gentlemen through a miracle. Yes, God speaks.

My wife is an amazing, sensitive woman who loves her Lord. One day she came to me and informed me we needed to go to the grocery store and buy some groceries. The Lord had told her that there was a family in need and the mother was asking for help. Off to the store we went. We proceeded to fill the cart with groceries. When we left the store she said we needed to drive to a small town about seven miles from where we lived. How she knew what street and what house is a mystery to me. I did not have a clue who this family was, and I am not sure that my wife did either, however, that was not important. The important thing was that she was obedient to her Lord. When we knocked, a young woman opened the door. My wife informed her that we had some groceries for her and would she mind if we brought them in. "Groceries? From whom?" the woman asked. My wife shared how the Lord had spoken to her and revealed that she had a need. The woman started crying. She invited us into her home, and through the tears said she wanted to show us something. She took us into the kitchen and proceeded to open her cabinets. They were all empty except for one can of chicken noodle soup which she was about to prepare for her two small children. She was going to go hungry. She had gone through some serious situations that completely drained her finances and she had nothing left to buy food. Out of desperation she asked the Lord for help. She did not know what else to do until aid came. God speaks. God spoke to my wife, and we were able to bless that family with enough groceries to last them until they could get back on their feet. God spoke to that woman through an amazing miracle.

We were leaving church after a powerful, refreshing service when my wife and I turned to each other and, at the same time, said we needed to go talk to a young couple who had just started coming to church. However, we needed to wait until the Lord released us to go. I thought that was interesting. Why would He have us wait? Several days later we both knew it was time. When they answered the knock on their door, they were pleasantly surprised to see us and they invited us in. Without delay I informed them that the Lord had sent us to them and I needed to share my testimony. As I began to share with them the problems I had created and the need to file for bankruptcy, the young lady began to cry and her husband simply sat there with a stunned look on his face.

Apparently the visitation pastor from the church had just left less than thirty minutes before we arrived. Unfortunately he was unable to offer them the solace or advice they so desperately needed because he could not relate to what they were going through. Before he left, he prayed with them and asked the Lord to send someone who could understand their circumstances and help them. Needless to say, the situation they faced was exactly what my wife and I had experienced. It was amazing how God gave them a sense of peace and confidence. They did not know what the next day was to hold, however, they knew that God was concerned if He would ask us to come. We were able to encourage them and let them know that, even in their darkest valley, the Lord was walking with them and He was in total control. That experience gave them the confidence and peace to sustain them through the entire ordeal. Their faith was energized because God was faithful and spoke to them through a simple answer to prayer. The last time I heard, they were working for their Lord as missionaries in Mexico.

What an awesome experience when one hears the voice of God. When God speaks, change happens. People are changed, situations are changed, lives are touched, faith explodes, God is glorified, all because of who He is. It wasn't Grandma Rapp. It wasn't my wife. It wasn't about me. The Lord spoke. He made the difference. We were simply willing servants who, a long time ago, had asked the Lord to "use us". Speak to our hearts, Lord. Tell us what You need us to do. He does, He did, and we trust that He will continue to. Now I realize that there will be those who have a problem with what I am sharing, or there may be those who attribute it to the fact that we are part of the "lucky ones", however, that is not the case. Luck has nothing to do with it. We do not have a special access card into the throne room of grace. It has nothing to do with who we are. It has everything to do with who He is. Grandma Rapp would have been the first one to tell you she was no one special. Matter of fact, she was amazed that the Lord would even want to use her with the life she lived BC (before Christ).

I was busy at work one afternoon when a young man approached me and asked if I would be willing to help him. I do not try to hide the fact that I love Jesus. There were some I worked with who considered me a religious fanatic and did not want anything to do with me. There were others who simply tolerated me, and two or three who had experienced the same freedom in Christ I had. The thing that amazed me, however, was the fact that when the nonbelievers found themselves in situations they could not handle, they would come and ask for help. In Stan's case, he was a member of a church that was suffocating under a conservative theology based upon doctrines of works. Their salvation was not found in a relationship with a loving God, but in an endless repetition of rituals and absolute obedience to a set of liturgical laws. Something happened, however, that changed all that. God spoke and twenty-two members of the congregation, including the pastor, invited Jesus into their lives as their Savior. The changes did not stop there. They went on a retreat at a small Kansas church camp and, horrors of horrors, they were all empowered by the Holy Spirit. Now what? They did not have a clue. These events did not fit in their theology. They were definitely outside of their box. After explaining their situation, he asked me if my wife and I would be willing to come and help them by explaining what had happened in a way they could all understand and relate to. After getting my pastor's blessings and encouragement, I informed him that we would be honored to share with them, however, God spoke very clearly and asked us not to say anything until the opportunity was presented. How strange, and yet that was His instructions. Okay, that was good enough for us.

It was about thirty miles from our house to the parsonage, and it took approximately forty-five minutes to get there. It was a great drive along the Illinois River. Out in the country. Fresh, clean air. You could just feel the presence of God going with us. We both knew that something special was going to happen that evening, however, never in our wildest imaginations could we have anticipated what God did. When we arrived, we were pleased to see that everyone else was already there. You could sense a feeling of expectancy. We were introduced and then spent a few minutes in worship with the people after which the pastor proceeded to set up a large chalk board with a number of words and diagrams. What followed was an intellectual, philosophical, scientific discussion on what the pastor thought had taken place. He used such words as pneuma, summa, id, ego, and others which I had no idea what they were or what they meant. That, however, was not surprising, because the things of God cannot be understood from a human perspective. It is impossible. The Apostle Paul tells us in I Corinthians 2:14. "The man without the Spirit does not accept the things that come from the Spirit of God, for they are foolishness to him, and he cannot understand them, because they are spiritually discerned." It takes faith. After being totally confused and bored for thirty minutes, the pastor said, "Now that we all understand what took place, let's pray before we go home." I am sitting on the piano bench with my wife thinking, "Lord, am I missing something?" The pastor could not pray. He was absolutely speechless. Every time he tried he would get tongue-tied and nothing would come out. Finally he quit trying and said, "Evidently there is someone else who has something to say." That was the opportunity the Lord had told us to wait for.

At that point my wife and I began to share a message on how simple it is to live in the Spirit and serve a loving, caring, awesome God. It is not complicated. There were four simple steps that the believers had to take in order to be in a position where they could hear from God and be used of God. First of all they needed to understand and believe that salvation and the empowerment of the Spirit cannot be earned. They are gifts from a God who loves you. They are not things that can be bartered for. The second thing the believer must do is believe that these gifts are given to each person individually. They are not corporate gifts. The third step is, just like any other gift, the believer needs to ask for them and accept them with a grateful heart. They are yours. Take them and benefit from them. In Matthew's Gospel chapter 7 verses 7-11 we read:

> "Ask and it will be given to you; seek and you will find; knock and the door will be opened to you. For everyone who asks

receives; he who seeks finds; and to him who knocks, the door will be opened. Which of you, if his son asks for bread, will give him a stone? Or if he asks for a fish, will give him a snake? If you, then, though you are evil, know how to give good gifts to your children, how much more will your Father in heaven give good gifts to those who ask Him?"

The fourth and final step is to use the gifts, live the gifts, and enjoy the gifts. If my wife would give me a very nice shirt and I would hang it in my closet, and every time I see it I would remark on what a nice gift it was, it would remain a nice gift and it would serve no useful purpose. You need to use that which God has given you. About that time a young lady spoke up and asked, "That seems awful simple, but how do you do it?" Since the human mind cannot understand or even receive the things of God, you must believe by faith that He will do what He says He will do. If we are to live by faith, then we must understand where faith comes from. Paul gives us the answer in his letter to the church in Rome. In Romans 10:17 we read, "So then faith cometh by hearing, and hearing by the Word of God." Another gentleman then asked, "Can we really understand the Word of God?" Jesus answers that question in The Gospel of John 8:31,32.

> "Then said Jesus to those Jews which believed on Him, if ye continue in My Word, then are ye My disciples indeed; and ye shall know the truth and the truth shall make you free."

Yes, you can understand the Word of God, however, it is not going to happen overnight. Jesus said we must continue in His Word. It is a process that begins when we accept Jesus as Lord and continues throughout our entire life. Paul reinforces this truth in I Corinthians 2:12,13

> "We have not received the spirit of this world but the Spirit who is from God, that we may understand what God has freely given us. This is what we speak, not in words taught us by human wisdom but in words taught by the Spirit, expressing spiritual truths in spiritual words."

A simple message. It was not complicated, and every one of them said that they were willing to give God a chance and accept His precious gifts by faith trusting that the Word of God would reveal the truth of what took place in their lives. In conclusion, or what we thought was conclusion, we asked the pastor and his wife if we could anoint them and pray for them. As we placed the oil on their foreheads and began to pray for them, the Holy Spirit gently laid them flat on their backs. Their people gathered around and began to pray over them. My wife and I retired to the piano bench where we had spent the majority of the evening and witnessed an outpouring of God that far surpassed anything that we had witnessed before or since. To our amazement, every one of the Gifts of the Spirit listed in I Corinthians 12 were manifested.

A word of prophecy was spoken over the pastor's wife. No one knew they had been trying hard to have a child for the previous six months to no avail. The word spoken declared that she was to become pregnant and would deliver a child at this same time next year. What made the prophecy interesting is the fact that she was told, if they remain strong in the Lord and the gifts they had received, he would be a blessing to them. If they turned their backs on the gifts that God had given them, he would be a curse. For a moment I had reservations over the last part of that prophecy, however, everyone rejoiced and began to give praise to God and worship Him in the spirit using beautiful spiritual languages. It had to be similar to what happened on the Day of Pentecost. It did not take long, however, when a woman with a bewildered look on her face turned to one of the gentlemen and asked, "What are you doing? You know exactly what you are saying." That got his attention. He grew up in New York in a Yiddish neighborhood and understood Hebrew. He was not worshiping in the Spirit. He was worshipping in his own understanding while speaking Hebrew. Without hesitation he asked God to forgive him and instantly a beautiful heavenly language began to pour out of him as tears streamed down his face. After a few minutes, he turned to another woman and pointed out an area in her lower back where she was experiencing a great deal of pain. "How did you know that?" she cried. "I haven't even told my husband about it yet." She did not have to. Jesus touched her and she was completely healed. Another man was delivered from the desire for cigarettes. The cravings totally gone. The ache in his stomach had disappeared. A young lady began to speak a powerful message in tongues and another followed with an interpretation. My wife confirmed the interpretation because it was exactly what the Spirit had shown her. Never in our wildest imaginations could my wife or I have orchestrated an evening like that. God, in His mercy and grace, showed Himself to be powerful and true. Why? Because a group of common, ordinary people just like you and me were hungry for God and the things of God. They were willing to take a chance and trust Him at His Word. There was absolutely no way my wife nor I could take credit for anything. We simply sat back and rejoiced over what we saw and heard. It was awesome.

I would like to say that everything turned out to be peaches and cream, but I cannot. The prophecy spoken over the pastor's wife came to pass. She became pregnant. All the signs indicated twins. The doctors said there were two heartbeats and they should prepare for two children. The prophecy said "a child" would be born. When the day came to deliver, a son was born. Just one child was born. There were no twins. The tragedy came when the pastor finally gave up because he could not comprehend the simplicity of what was taught that evening. It could not possibly be that easy, he reasoned. There had to be a rational explanation beyond what my wife and I shared with them. He could not accept it in its simplicity and drifted away from what God had established in their lives. He left the ministry and returned to his father's farm in Missouri. I have not heard from him since, however, it grieves me to say that their son turned out to be a curse to them. How do I know? Because God spoke and said it would be so if they turned their backs on what they had been given. The one hope I have is that they realized the error of their ways and asked for God's forgiveness. If that is the case, then their son became a real blessing to them. That sounds a lot better. Let's believe that is what happened. That small group of believers went on to form a wonderful new church and within two years had grown to over 200 people with a building of their own. To God goes the glory.

Believe me. As hard as it may be to accept or understand what I am sharing with you, it is the reality of walking and living in the Spirit. These are not whimsical spiritual fantasies. These events happened. They have happened and they will continue to happen where people are seeking the truth of who God is and what He has to offer. It is not about a group of 22 new believers. It is all about Jesus and the fact that He is eager to show Himself faithful, true, loving, and willing to respond to those who truly seek Him. Proverbs 8:17 declares: "I love those who love Me, and those who seek Me find Me." Are you seeking Him? Are you willing to move out from under the oppression of endless traditions and the stifling pressure of trying to obey liturgical laws and obligations and simply say, "Lord, I may not understand it yet, however, I am willing to give it a try. I will believe that You are who You say You are. I am willing to accept the precious gifts that You provide for those who are willing to believe. I am willing to study Your word and, by faith, live by every precept it teaches. I am willing to trust you and believe that Your Word will indeed set me free." If that is your confession, then expect a miracle, because God will move in your life. You will never be the same. Matter of fact, you will never even have a desire to stay the same. Life with Jesus is an awesome adventure, and it is available for all those who understand and believe that ...

God loves the common person!

Jesus Is Alive

I have often heard that a person is extremely fortunate if, during his lifetime, he could count one or two individuals as dear friends. I guess my wife and I have been overly blessed. We have had the privilege of enjoying the great friendships of several wonderful couples. Few, however, have had the impact on us that Dick and Dee have. I can remember times in ministry, not too long ago, where the pressures seemed to be overwhelming and Dick was there with an uplifting word of encouragement or a tidbit of godly wisdom. Several years ago my wife and I had the privilege of going to Hawaii with them, and we had a marvelous time enjoying the beauty of God's creation. Dick has been blessed with a successful ministry that reaches out to hurting pastors or those in the ministry who have been wounded, bruised, or those who are simply worn out by the constant warfare. For those of you who are in ministry, you can relate to what I am saying. For those who are not, let it suffice to say that serving the Lord can be, and often is a challenge, however, the rewards are more than worth it even if the pay isn't.

In this story we want to focus our attention on Dee. I have known few women, if any, that display as gentle and as loving a character as hers. From all appearances her life sails on a calm, beautiful sea, however, that was not always the case. You may say that her early years were a nightmare. She was forced to deal with situations and circumstances that literally robbed her of her innocence and her childhood. For years she tried her best to win the approval of her father. Instead of acceptance she received rejection and abuse. It is difficult to appreciate or understand the trauma and the effects of that type of trauma on a delicate young life. The sense of rejection, failure, and worthlessness replaced an understanding of love. These are the scars that you cannot leave in the past as you grow. She survived the tragic environment of her youth. However, the feelings of insignificance, the hurts, and the rejections not only survived with her, they served to form a very strong defensive mechanism. It was difficult for her to let her guard down especially when it came to relationships with men. How could she trust them? How could she know for sure that they were not trying to take advantage of her? It was difficult. These issues got in the way until a suave, debonair gentleman came into her life. Dick was different. He seemed to care in a way that was inconsistent with how she thought men would care. His motives were different. It was not a matter of what he could get from her. It was a matter of actually loving her for who she was. To her, that was unique. That was not only a surprise, it was a challenge.

Eventually his consistency in his commitment to her won her heart and they were married.

    Surely those who have similar stories to tell realize and understand that change is difficult. Matter of fact, in your own strength, it is next to impossible to put the effects of the kind of trauma Dee experienced out of your mind, let alone your relationships. It was a difficult time for her. So many questions. So few answers. Surely somewhere there was someone who could help her through her past hurts and confusions. She came to the point where she had convinced herself that she was an unfit mother and an unfit wife. Something had to happen or else she was going to leave Dick and the children. Divorce frightened her, but what else could she do? The battle inside of her was raging and there simply seemed to be no other solution.

    Now understand that there are no coincidences with God and His timing is perfect. It was at this time in her life when her husband made arrangements for her to go to a ladies retreat at a local church in the Detroit area. It was a cold, wet December weekend and she went with apprehensions, not knowing what to expect. Hopefully she would find the answers she so desperately sought. That Friday was a very restless night. The wine she longed for was not available, neither was the sleep her body craved. The next morning she was to meet with a staff counselor who she hoped could help her. As she finished her story, she look at the man and noticed tears in his eyes. Confused, she wondered, "What did I do?" Instead of having answers, he revealed that his story was parallel to hers and he could not help her because he was still searching for the same answers himself. In fact, he asked her to come back and share with him if she ever did find the answers. Now wait a minute. This is not how it is supposed to happen. If she could not get the answers from a man of the cloth, where are they going to come from? Unfortunately events continued to go downhill that morning. The women were asked to complete a self-evaluation test. It was designed to encourage the individual. Instead of encouragement, Dee's test seemed to reinforce the negative feelings she brought with her. Her test revealed that she could have been considered a "basket case". It became apparent as the day progressed that there was no hope for her.

That evening, with a sense of desperation compelling her, she decided to visit the chapel. The lights were dimmed and she was all alone. As she knelt before the altar, her attention was drawn to a huge twenty-foot cross with the figure of Christ upon it. Something was different. Why wasn't His head on His breast like all the other crosses she had seen? His head was raised. He was looking toward heaven.

All of a sudden a sense of joy consumed her as she realized that He was not dead. Jesus was alive. That revelation so consumed her that she began to talk to Him out loud. "Oh Lord, what do I do?" In the stillness of the chapel, God began to speak. Pictures from her past began to parade before her. She saw the faces of the people who had hurt her, rejected her, and abused her. At the same time, she felt a compelling urge to forgive them, which she quickly did. Then she suddenly saw the figure of her father. "No, God. I cannot do that, God. How can I forgive him after all that he did to me?", and yet, she knew that nothing more would happen until she came to grips with her emotions and forgave him. "Jesus," she cried out, "help me forgive him. She knew that it had to be the Grace of God working in her that gave her the courage she needed, because all the forces of her emotions were ready to do battle. They all screamed, "How can you forgive him?" And yet she did. What a tremendous step she took. God was not finished with her, however. She saw herself as if in a mirror as a sinner, unclean. All the others she saw were those who sinned against her. She was the victim, yet now, she was the sinner, and it was plain to her it was her sins that helped place Jesus on that cross. What was she to do? Fear began to creep into her when suddenly music came into the room. For the first time she heard the song "Amazing Grace." The words consumed her. She was wretched. She was lost. She was blind and she knew it. In desperation she cried out, "Jesus, save me!"

That evening, in a quiet little chapel in Detroit, Michigan, Dee completely surrendered her life to the Lord Jesus Christ. It seemed as if a huge weight had been lifted off her shoulders. A peace that she had been so desperately searching for, and yet unable to find, seemed to overwhelm her. Once again God spoke and told her that her marriage was going to be totally healed. Finally, the answers she had been searching for were right there before her. Well, at least most of them, for God was still not done with her. That night was the first night in a long time where she slept soundly all night with no nightmares. The next morning she arose with a joy in her heart and a bounce in her step that she had never experienced before. Man did not have the answers. Man could not help her. She could not help herself, however, a loving and merciful God heard her cry and said, "I can help" and help He did. All the rejection, all the hurt from the abuse, all the fear, all the distrust, all the loneliness, all the nightmares, and all the poor self image were gone. In their place was a peace, and a joy, and a confidence that could not be explained. When she returned home the next day, it was obvious that something had happened. She was not the same. When Dick first saw her, even before she said a word, he knew there was a difference, and it was not a difference he liked.

For months afterward, Dick and Dee's counselor questioned her and did everything they could to convince her that what she had experienced was not good. They tried their best to use past hurts to get a reaction, but it did not work. It was as if God had placed a protective hedge around her. They could not prove her wrong. She had experienced something wonderful and she knew it. She was excited. She was healed. She was forgiven. She knew that she was a new woman free from her past. It was the first time in her life that she felt in control of her circumstances and nothing could back her into a corner. She knew what happened was real. She had literally experienced II Corinthians 5:17, "Therefore, if anyone is in Christ, he is a new creation; the old has gone, the new has come."

Even though there was a tremendous transformation, it was not long until she realized that this "newness" business was a process. There were issues that she had to work on. For instance, even after her chapel experience, she had trouble quitting smoking. Even though she tried her best to quit, she kept going back to her cigarettes. None of the over-the-counter remedies seemed to work. Her children tried to help by hiding them from her, and threatening to smoke themselves when they got older. You know, the old "If it is good enough for you, it is good enough for us" threat. It did not work. The only thing that seemed to work was when she became desperate she cried out to the Lord for help. The desire was taken from her. The cravings were gone with no signs of withdrawal, even though she had smoked for years. Man, temptation is a nasty enemy. After several weeks of freedom, she returned to her cigarettes which she had hidden in the freezer just in case. At night she would hurry up and sneak a few puffs, get rid of it, brush her teeth, and rinse her mouth so that Dick would not know what she was doing. No one knew, life was good, and she had the best of both worlds until guilt began to accompany each trip to the freezer. "Why was I doing this, Lord?" How could she testify to the goodness and mercy of a loving God when she was holding onto something she knew was not pleasing to Him?

It seems at times that God has a sense of humor. As she sat there struggling with the guilt, the Lord began to speak to her in a dream. She saw herself looking out of her front room window at twenty full garbage cans. The garbage truck came and emptied nineteen and left one. What could that mean? The next morning she explained to her husband what she had seen, and he began to chuckle. "Those twenty garbage cans represent the number of cigarettes in a pack. The one can represents that cigarette you are smoking every night," he told her. Dee began to cry.

Dick had known all along what was going on, and he still loved her and did not condemn her. She quickly repented and was once and for all totally delivered from the addiction to nicotine. She no longer had a desire to smoke.

The final chapter of her amazing story, at least for our purpose, began four months later on a cold April morning. She had made arrangements to go to a small retreat center in Clear Lake, Michigan, for a weekend gathering of her woman friends. Once again the Holy Spirit had been working in her. She had been baptized as an infant, however, she saw in the Word of God that she was to "repent and be baptized."

> "Peter replied, 'Repent and be baptized, every one of you in the name of Jesus Christ for the forgiveness of your sins. And you will receive the gift of the Holy Spirit. The promise is for you and your children and for all who are far off – for all whom the Lord will call." II Corinthians 2:38,39

"It is impossible for an infant to repent. How could an infant believe on the Lord Jesus for salvation?" she reasoned. She knew that she needed to take that step and be baptized as a public declaration of what took place on the inside, however, where was she going to do it? Her church was certainly not the place. Their traditions did not allow for adult baptism. The desire continued to build. When she approached the retreat leaders, they were somewhat surprised because no one had ever requested it before. It was early April. The weather was cold. There was still ice floating on the surface of the lake. That might be a problem! That did not matter to her. She knew that God had led her there to be baptized. One of the leaders asked her if she had been baptized as an infant. "That is sufficient," he informed her. Not to be deterred, she shared a dream that she had which convinced her of the need to be baptized as an adult. Finally, after much haggling, the leader consented and announced that there would be a baptism service later that day. Six other people raised their hands and said they also wanted to be included. God was definitely doing something, including breaking down traditional barriers. The time came. Everyone was ready, and they proceeded to the lake. As they started to enter the frigid water, a cloud of small gnat-sized insects swarmed around them. The leader commanded them to leave and they did. Once again they started into the water only to see a pack of wild dogs come charging out of the woods directly at them. Again the leader rebuked them in the name of Jesus and immediately they turned and went scurrying away. It seemed like all the forces of hell were against them, however, with determined resolve, into the water they went. It seemed like she was under the frigid water for a long time, however, when she came out something awesome happened. She could actually feel "the fear of man" leave her. She knew that her life would never be the same because of this simple act of obedience.

By the time the retreat had ended and it was time to leave for home, the weather had turned nasty. It was a 3-1/2 hour journey and it was late. It would not be an easy trip. The women stopped outside of Clear Lake to fill up their car. After looking over the situation, they decided that God would be sufficient and would grant them a safe journey. As they entered Interstate 94 heading toward Detroit, they began to sing and praise and worship Jesus. It seemed as if a mist had engulfed the car, and a golden belt surrounded them. It was a great time of peace. The presence of God filled the car. Suddenly the mist disappeared as they pulled into the driveway of Dee's house. She was the first one to be dropped off. Wait a minute. This is impossible. We just left the gas station. What happened? They left the retreat center less than forty minutes ago. How could they be home already? Dick was so surprised to see them home so early he went and checked the gas gauge. The tank was still full!!

Now wait a minute or maybe even two. Those things do not happen. Why not? God is a miracle-working God. Jesus performed countless miracles while He walked the earth. Matter of fact, Acts 8:38-40 tells us about a similar happening. The Holy Spirit had directed Philip to go to an Ethiopian eunuch who was struggling with the Word of God and explain it to him. The eunuch not only believed on the Lord, he asked to be baptized.

> "And he gave orders to stop the chariot. Then both Philip and the eunuch went down into water and Philip baptized him. When they came up out of the water, the spirit of the Lord suddenly took Philip away, and the eunuch did not see him again, but went on his way rejoicing. Philip, however, appeared at Azotus and traveled about, preaching the Gospel in all the towns until he reached Caesarea."

What makes you think He cannot do the same now? He not only can, He does. He is still a miracle-working God. He has not changed and He will never change. If you are honest with yourself, you can look back and identify times in your life when God touched you in a miraculous way. It may not have been as dramatic as the miracle that took place in

Dee's life and the lives of her friends, however, a miracle just the same. It may have been as subtle as a kind word from a stranger at a time in your life when a kind word was needed. It may have been a sack of groceries when the cupboards were bare, or a warm coat when the weather turned cold, or a new shirt when the buttons fell off the one you were wearing. It may have been a close encounter when an accident seemed imminent.

"I can't think of a time in my life when something like that happened." Well, that is not God's fault. He is willing and able to work on your behalf if you simply believe and give Him a chance. Matter of fact, there are times when He will show compassion and work on your behalf even though you do not know Him. "Well I do not believe in miracles. They were only seen in the early days of the church." That is sure foolishness. Why would you limit what God can do? If He spoke the worlds into existence, created you, and breathed life into you, why would you be so foolish to assume that He is unable to make a difference now? Maybe it is time that we reevaluate how we feel about Jesus and what He is able to do or not to do. If your traditions do not make room for the miracle-working power of a loving, caring, awesome, capable God, then maybe your traditions need to change. It is not difficult. It is not complicated. It is as simple as coming to the same realization that Dee came to when she realized that . . .

God loves the common person!

I Must Be The Best

I met a young family several years ago that literally swept me off my feet. If there was some way I could adopt them for my own, I would. They are a beautiful example of what I believe a family should be because they are so full of life and love for each other. Paul loves to work with children, and it is a good thing because he spends his days in a classroom teaching. Julie is a stay-at-home mom who homeschools their four children, all under twelve years old. The entire family loves the Lord and serves Him faithfully. Periodically they will go to a local coffee house and play their instruments and sing. They are champions in the fight against abortion and are very active in the Right to Life organization. If you would look at them, they would be as close to an ideal family as one could find.

It was not always that easy or that ideal. Paul would be the first to tell you that there was a great battle in his life he had to overcome. His story is unlike those I have shared with you up till now. There wasn't any earth shaking event that convinced him he needed to accept Jesus. There were no miraculous healings or awesome dreams or visions. It was not a matter of hearing the voice of God in his greatest moment of need. It was not any of that, however, the battle that raged in his life was serious and potentially dangerous. His battle was not with outside forces. He was not facing a tragedy in his family. He was not being consumed with alcohol or drugs. His battle was with himself. Is that a unique situation? Absolutely not. In all reality the greatest warfare we face is not with other people or trying situations and circumstances. Our greatest battles are on the inside. There are five voices we are going to listen to and only five. We are going to listen to other people, our past, the devil, the Lord, or our emotions. Of the five voices the one that screams the loudest is our emotions. Our emotions affect every action and reaction, relationship, and decision that we may have to deal with. Our emotions literally mold us into who we are. Paul's story is not unique. I know there are many who will be able to relate to what he struggled with and what he put himself through. Let Paul tell his story in his own words, and let it be a word of encouragement for those who are struggling with their emotions.

Hello there. My name is Paul and, if I were to define my early life, I would have to take you to the land of make believe and introduce you to Mother Goose. All those children! How in the world was she able to control all of them? I have four children under twelve. They are awesome kids; however, there are times when they can be a hand full. My parents had five of us little rug rats, and when the youngest was born the oldest was only five years old. If I were to describe those days I would have to rely on such phrases as organized chaos, instant pandemonium, or constant competition. It was not easy especially when I was the unfortunate one who fell right in the middle. It seemed like the oldest brother got all the best toys to play with, if for no other reason, he was bigger than the rest of us and simply took them. My baby brother seemed to get all the attention. All he had to do was cry and my parents were right there for him. If I cried, I got in trouble. Man, life did not seem fair.

I do not know if I was capable of making a life changing decision at the age of three or not. All I do know is at a very early age I needed to be "better than". I was tired of being left out. I wanted my parents to pay more attention to me. I know I could not simply throw a fit to get attention, because that was not the kind of attention I craved. Therefore, when we colored, my picture had to be the best. I worked hard at making sure that I stayed within the lines. I worked hard at making my pictures actually look like what I said they were. If we played games, I played to win. If we chased each other around, I had to be the fastest runner. If we played sports, I had to hit the ball the farthest, or kick the ball the highest, or make the longest basket. Now do not tell me a child cannot be driven. I know better. I had to be the best. I wanted the recognition that came with being the best.

My efforts began to pay dividends as early as elementary school. When I entered an art contest, my drawings always won first place. When I started playing sports in school, I was always the one they could count on to make the winning basket, score the winning touchdown, or knock in the winning run. The drive and desire to excel even extended into the area of music. When I began drum lessons, it did not take long and I was considered the best drummer in the band. Hey, this is cool. Everyone noticed me. When teams were chosen for different sports, I was always the first one chosen. I was somebody. I was important. I did not play second fiddle to anyone now. That may have been true; however, it was not a healthy attitude for someone not yet in high school. Matter of fact, it is not a healthy attitude no matter how old you are. I became obsessed with achieving and winning.

Instead of being content and happy, however, I found myself constantly fighting a fear of losing and a sense of insecurity. What if someone came along who was better than I was, stronger than I was, or faster than I was? How could I live up to people's expectations? I had to have their approval and I was convinced that I would not if I failed to be the best. I had to be the best in order to be important and noticed. I was convinced that, if I could stay the best, everything else would fall into place. People would not be able to do anything but like me. How shallow that reasoning seems now as I look back on those days. Instead of drawing people to me, I ended up doing just the opposite. I began to avoid any activity where I thought there might be even a slim chance of coming in second. I avoided relationships if I thought, even for a moment, that there might be rejection. Instead of finding great joy and a sense of accomplishment in what I was doing, I often found myself consumed with the pressure and stress of striving. Even more debilitating were the disdain and disgust I felt toward those I thought were not as talented as I was. I became critical, especially toward those I saw as a threat to me. Mister Popularity found himself becoming a very lonely individual. Why? It was not consistent with what other people saw. They thought I was cool, however, under the surface, I was not the nice all-American kid next door. I did not care what people thought. I cared about one thing and that was myself and my success.

What a relief when high school graduation finally arrived. I made it. Finally I did not have to prove myself any more. I did not have to keep trying to convince others how great I was. All that stress and pressure and striving finally paid off. I was somebody. I was Mister Popularity. I even had a music scholarship from a very reputable university.

The hard part was over. The rest of the story would be a snap. A little naïve? I think so because I was not prepared for what happened next. My first year of college was anything but a cakewalk. The stress and pressure were almost overwhelming, and I even considered dropping out. In my way of thinking, that would have been far better than failing. There were times when I honestly thought I was in over my head.

I was in trouble and I knew it. I did not have the answers. It was during this period of my life when I began to reconsider what I believed about God, because my beliefs were obviously not working. My family attended church regularly, and they expected me to go with them. It was something they believed was important and necessary. So I went. However, church to me was extremely boring. I guess the only reason I went was because I was convinced that the only way to get into heaven was to be a good person and to attend church. By doing those two things, God was obligated to let me in. I had no room for a personal relationship with Him in my theology. I began to spend time in His Word especially in the Book of Psalms. I found out some very interesting and cool things about myself and my God. I guess the greatest revelation came when I realized that God has placed legitimate requirements on those who would come to Him. I began to realize that those expectations did not include going to church, reading the Word, or even praying. Now do not misunderstand me. Those things are all very important and should never be ignored, however, I found that His requirements were simple. I needed to come to the point where I realized that I was a sinner, and that the penalty for my sins was eternal separation from God. If I was going to qualify for heaven, I had to do something about this sin issue. That is where the struggle really began.

Even though I had the head knowledge and I knew what I had to deal with, it was very difficult because of my struggles with a sense of low self-esteem, depression, and the thought of possible failure. I could not shake the need to be in control. I still had a fanatical desire to do things my way. I found myself manipulating the Word. I came to the point where I considered God a good counselor and the Word as a moral road map. Fortunately, however, I did not stop reading His Word, and I eventually came to the point where I saw in John 10:10 "My sheep hear My voice." Now wait a minute. I was not hearing any voice. Did that mean I was not one of His? What was missing? That is when the Holy Spirit finally began to speak to me and reveal that I needed more than head knowledge. It was not good enough to know about Him. I needed a personal relationship with the Lord Jesus Christ, and the only way that was going to happen was for me to acknowledge my sins and ask Him to forgive them. The next step was to simply invite Him into my life to be my Lord and Savior. Finally, in the spring of 1989, I came to the point where I was tired of doing things my way. I did not have to be the best anymore. I did not need man's approval or acceptance any more. I simply said, "Okay God, from now on I am going to do it Your way."

What a difference that decision has made in my life. For the first time I was able to see what my emotions and decisions were doing to me and those close to me. I was able, finally, to not only forgive, but to ask for forgiveness from those I had offended or hurt. I actually fell in love with people, and I found myself rejoicing with them when they achieved success in their lives instead of feeling jealousy. People became important, special, and valuable in their own rights instead of tools and assets to be used to get what I wanted. I absolutely adore my wife and my children. They are not simply badges of honor, they are my very life and my purpose in living. God has truly blessed me. If there is one thing in this amazing transition that brings me true joy, it is the desire I now have to reach out and help those I see who are less fortunate than I. That is truly amazing, considering my life revolved around me and what I wanted. People did not hold much value unless they had what I needed. Now I find tremendous satisfaction in reaching out to those who need help. I have a special burden for those precious children who face the horrible possibility of abortion. To me there is no greater joy than knowing that something I said or did might have changed a mind and saved one of those precious lives.

Have I arrived? Am I at that point in my life where I would consider everything perfect? Absolutely not. I am simply a "Christian under construction" and God, in His mercy and faithfulness, is continuing to change me and shape me into His image. I no longer deal with feelings of insecurity or failure. I have learned to place my confidence and my trust in the Lord Jesus Christ. His Word is true and cannot fail; that is why I consider Philippians 1:6 my special mantra. "He who began a good work in you will carry it on to completion until the day of Christ Jesus."

If you have been touched by what I have shared, and can relate to what I put myself through, take heart. I am no one special. I do not have any special claims to God's mercy and grace. There are tens of thousands who have experienced or are experiencing the same emotions, frustrations, despair, low self esteem, and fears of failure that I did. If God would take the time and invest the effort to help me turn my life around, I know He will do the same for you.

Simply give Him a chance. That is all I did and it led me to the awesome revelation that . . .

God loves the common person!

He Will Love Me Or Else

We all face them every day. There is no running from them. There is no hiding from them. Every thing we do is affected by them. We are shaped and molded by them. Matter of fact, we are a product of them. Far too often we find ourselves frustrated, confused, angry, hurting, and fighting a battle with our emotions because we do not count the cost before we make decisions. Whether we want to admit it or not, there is a price to pay for the decisions we make, and unfortunately that price is invariably paid after the fact.

We have been blessed with the addition of a young lady to our lives . She is a joy to be around. She loves life. She loves her Lord. However, up until recently her life has been anything but tranquil. Her decisions have caused her to take some rather twisted turns in her life, and the price she has been asked to pay is more than most people would be able to cope with. Matter of fact, it has almost been more than she was able to cope with. I have asked if she would share with us her story and how her decisions brought her to a point of utter desperation. I know that there are many who have gone or are going through situations very similar to hers. Let her story be a word of encouragement and hope to you.

From a very early age the only thing I wanted or ever thought about was being a wife and a mother. I had a fanatical desire to have someone that I could love unconditionally, and who would return that love in like manner. I was not sure, however, what that "love" really was. You see, my parents loved my brothers and me, however, there seemed to be conditions on that love and I always felt like I never measured up to their expectations. I was never quite good enough. I could never quite achieve what I thought were their goals for me. What did I do? I made some poor decisions. I simply gave up trying and began seeking friends who would accept me for who I was. Unfortunately, I rebelled and turned to drugs and alcohol. At the time it seemed to be the cool thing to do. I did not have to prove myself to anyone. Simply get high. What was there to worry about?

It was not long, however, when I came to the point where I realized I wasn't even good at partying. There was no excitement. There was nothing of any value in what I was doing, and it resulted in honestly believing that my life had little or no meaning. I felt like a nonentity. I was desperate. I needed someone to take me out of this spiral that was leading to nowhere. I needed a man. I needed a husband. I never wanted a career. I never desired fame or fortune. I longed for a relationship that could give my life meaning and a purpose. I became so desperate I began to look, and unfortunately, I made some more bad decisions by looking for "broken" men in the only world I had known. I would go from bar to bar seeking that "Mr. Right."

It was degrading. It was discouraging until that fateful Easter Sunday in 1979. I finally found him. I finally found Mr. Right who would love me for who I was and who would give me the child I so desperately desired. It did not make any difference that he was just coming off a divorce. It did not make any difference that he was simply seeking someone to replace his wife. It did not make a difference that he had a two-year-old daughter he needed help with. All I know is he was the one I had been looking for. A week later we were living together and four months after that we were married in my parents' church. It did not matter that he was an alcoholic. I understood what that meant and I could deal with it and I could help him change.

Unfortunately, it was not that easy. Before our first anniversary he entered his first 30-day treatment program. I did everything I could think of to help him stop drinking. I do not know how much booze I poured down the drain. That did not work. I tried to be his drinking buddy, thinking I could bring some sense of moderation into his life. That did not work. I even gave up drinking myself hoping he would see what it was doing to him. That did not work. I tried to change him. I could not. It came down to the point where his boss finally forced the issue and off to rehab he went again. It was either change or lose his job. That is what he needed. That would sober him up and when he came out, I would put the clamps on him and all would be well. It worked for awhile, however, five years later he was back in rehab and I was even more determined to keep him clean and sober. It was all up to me now. I know he needed me to show him the "errors of his ways" and keep him on the straight and narrow. I had waited far too long to have someone love me and by God he was going to shape up or else! I am glad that no one asked me what the "or else" was. I am really not sure. There had never been a divorce in my family and I was not going to be responsible for the first. All I did know I was going to be "super wife" and I was going to replace whatever drove him to the alcohol.

Once again decision time. How was I going to replace that motivation to drink? Both of us had very good jobs. We had plenty of money. I had taken control of the finances because he could not be trusted. I knew what I was going to do. I bought snow-mobiles and motorcycles and a nice boat. "Things" - that was what he needed. He needed things to keep himself occupied and away from the bottle. We had a fancy house with an immaculate yard. There wasn't a weed in sight. We had a bunch of "stuff". Matter of fact, we had far more than we needed or could justify, however, it seemed to be working. He was staying sober. We were fortunate to meet some great people who became very good friends. We were respected in our neighborhood. We both were very successful in our professions. My husband became known as one of the best in his field of endeavor. Finally a sense of normalcy came into our lives. We even became best of friends and enjoyed doing things together. I honestly believe that we had fallen in love with each other. Times were good. I finally had that man who would love me.

The years passed and no matter how happy I was I could never quite say I was content. There was still a huge void in my life. No matter how many things we had, I still did not have a child. I wanted a baby. Matter of fact, I wanted a baby even more than I wanted a loving husband. I knew that I would never be complete until I had a child I could call my own. So many years of trying and yet nothing. That is when I started talking to God. I had gone to church as a young girl. It was the same church my husband and I were married in. Unfortunately the congregation went through a horrible split over the issue of building a new sanctuary. It was awful and if that was what religion was all about, I did not want any part of it. I always knew that there was a God. I did not know Him, however, maybe He would help me. Nothing else had worked.

Why, God? Why won't You give me a baby. Haven't I proven myself yet? Haven't I kept my husband sober all these years? Surely by now I have qualified. How about if I quit smoking, God? You know I will "if" You let me have a baby. Lord, I know I drink, but You know I am not like my husband. If You give me a baby I will quit that, too. I begged and I pleaded and I made promise after promise. Where are You, God? Month after month. Year after agonizing year. Nothing. God, do You even know I am here? Do You care? Have I done too many wrong things in my life? All those men I slept with, all the drugs, all the drinking, all the lies, and stealing and cheating. Is that why, God. If You are going to hold them against me, God, I will never qualify for a child. God that is not fair. Once again I slip into that area of not quite being good enough. It seems to be the story of my life.

Desperation? Yes. For eighteen years I tried and there was nothing until I reached forty years old and then the miracle of all miracles. I was pregnant. I was going to have a baby. I cannot begin to describe the excitement I felt until I miscarried. That's not fair, God. That is cruel. How could You do that to me? The darkest time of my life until the sun began to shine once again two months later. Finally I was pregnant and this time all went well. I gave birth to a beautiful, healthy baby girl. Finally I was complete. After all those years I had the desires of my heart. I had a husband who loved me and a child I could call my own. I was so happy. I was consumed with being the best mother I could possibly be. I was so focused on my girl I did not see storm clouds gathering in my husband's life. I worked so hard at keeping him on the straight and narrow and yet when my daughter came along I let down my guard.

Why doesn't he smile any more? You would think that he would be elated with the baby. He also waited eighteen years. Where was he? What was he doing ? One day the phone rang and it was my husband.

"They let me go today, I lost my job."

"Where are you? Please come home. We need you."

"Soon. I will be home soon."

Hours went by. Hours turned into days. Where was he? What will we do? What has happened to him? He does not come home and desperation begins to take over. There had to be a reason. What could it possibly be?

    I will never forget the day I went into his garage to look for whatever it was that was destroying him. I was convinced that somewhere in the garage I would find the answer. He would spend hours out there and yet nothing seemed to be getting done. I searched and I searched and found nothing until I came to an old humidifier that was sitting in one of the corners. When I removed the top, I absolutely freaked out and ran back into the house. I was shaking and very frightened. It must have been ten minutes before I could make myself go back. The entire bottom portion of the humidifier was loaded with syringes. I had never seen a syringe outside of the doctor's office. I removed them one by one and counted over one hundred . What in the world was going on? There was a set of metal storage lockers at one end of the garage. Several times I had asked my husband what was in them and he kept telling me they were locked and he did not have the key and could not open them. He did not know what was in them. That was not going to stop me now. I was on a mission to get to the bottom of what was happening. A hammer and a crowbar and a few minutes of hard labor soon had the locks off and the cases open. The first case held dozens of liquor bottles, some of them partially full and others empty. The second case held papers. Lots of papers. Credit card statements from cards that were paid off and now were open again. Cards from J.C.Pennys, Sears, and Home Depot that were all maxed out. There were bank statements showing that our accounts were empty. Even the baby's college fund account was empty. My husband was treasurer of a trades association group and the association's accounts were also empty. I walked right into a nightmare. This cannot be happening. How could I have missed this? I returned to the house and began a very thorough search and found matches, spoons and empty foils in a spare bedroom. I called a gentleman I knew who had been involved in drugs at one time and even served time in prison. I had my suspicions and yet when he told me it was heroin, it felt like my world suddenly collapsed around me.

When he finally did show up, I confronted him. What I did not realize was after a back injury and surgery he had become addicted to pain killers. He began to manipulate the doctors in order to continue with the prescriptions. From there things began to spiral out of control. That is when he lost his job. Evidently he had been warned several times by his bosses. I did not know that. I was told there were cutbacks. All I know is that I watched my husband slide deeper and deeper into depression and we began to drift further and further apart. I could not understand what he was trying to prove. Why can't he get his lazy hind end off the couch and get another job? All I did was nag and push and watch him get sicker and sicker. I had no idea what was going on. No one told me. Those he worked with assumed I knew he had a problem. Was I not his wife? Should I not be aware if he was having problems? What I knew was I had a child and I was so consumed with her I did not see my husband's life falling apart.

What followed was the infamous trilogy of those who are hooked on drugs. First came the denial. They are not mine. I am keeping them for a friend. I am trying to help him quit. That did not work so then came the admittance. Okay, they are mine, but I can quit any time I want. That did not work. Then came the blame. It is the doctor's fault. They are the ones who got me hooked on the painkillers. Life became a constant repetition of detox and relapse, detox and relapse, detox and relapse. Every time he chose to return to his drugs, I felt like he was choosing them over his child and me. No matter what happened, I knew I had to remain strong for no other reason than my child. I am all she had. How could this be happening? I guess I wasn't quite the "super wife" I thought I was. Once again I found myself coming up short of expectations.

It was difficult, and the only one I thought I could rely on was a very close friend who had recently moved away. I would call her and cry on her shoulder and she kept telling me "All you need is a personal relationship with Jesus Christ." "Tammy, you do not understand. He did all these horrible things to me.." "All you need is a relationship with Jesus Christ." "Will you stop that? Can't you see I am hurting?"

There came a time, however, when I was desperate and needed to talk to someone so I called her. While talking to her I began to hurt so bad I honestly thought I was going to die, and I simply fell to my knees and cried out, "God, I cannot do it any more, help me please." It was incredible. I felt the tightness in my chest lift and the pain in my heart cease, and I heard Tammy on the other end of the phone say, "that's right, you cannot do it yourself, but God can if you let Him. Just ask Him into your heart." That was the day I asked Jesus Christ into my life. That is the day I turned over total control of my life to Him. For the first time in my life I began to live.

It has not been easy. My husband had to pay the price. We ended up getting a divorce and he went to prison where he served time for possession and theft. He had accumulated over $60,000 in credit card drug debt in three months. We lost the house, the boat, and all our "things" when we filed for bankruptcy. All those things had done nothing for us. There was no joy or peace or healing in them. They just took up space. So much gone and yet, I still have so much left. Even though I lost a husband, he left me with a precious, beautiful little girl who is rapidly growing into a very pretty young lady. I am so proud of her. The most important thing I found in the midst of all the hurt and pain and confusion was the one thing that was really missing in my life, and that was a relationship with a God who showed Himself faithful.

It has been six years since that darkest hour, and it still hurts when I think about what happened. It has been very difficult for me to even share with you what happened. The wounds still seem so fresh. At first I refused because I was still not ready to bring that period of my life to closure, however, I trust and believe that this testimony will be a time of healing for me. I made some foolish decisions in my life and I had to pay the price for them; however, I no longer trust in my own judgment. I now have a Savior who walks with me and I am learning to listen to Him for advice.

If what I have shared with you is speaking to you, and you are in the midst of situations that are tearing your world apart, please stop making those poor decisions like I did. Do the one thing that made a difference in my life and ask the Lord Jesus Christ to come into your life and be your Savior. Ask Him to forgive you for all the mistakes and bad decisions you have made and He will. I have found Him to be faithful and true. He has never let me down. He can bring hope and peace and joy into the midst of the storms of your life. He can show you what true love is. It is more than I can comprehend at times, however, I am so thankful for His mercy and grace toward me when I absolutely did not deserve them.

My daughter and I are now a team and we walk together. It amazes me how much God has done in my life, however, it amazes me even more to see what He is doing in my daughter. I cannot wait to see Jesus face to face and thank Him for His undying love, His perseverance in calling out to me, and His patience in waiting until I could finally hear His voice. I have no idea what the future may hold for my daughter and me, however, as I look forward to tomorrow, I thank God that He is continuing to hide the hurts, the pain, the fear, and loneliness in His great love. I am so thankful that my daughter and I have come to that awesome revelation that . . .

God loves the common person!

Will You Trust Me?

I have met so many people who have a relationship with the Lord Jesus and yet they are struggling. They question. They complain. They walk around with disappointment written all over their faces. There is no joy and very little victory in their lives. Why? Psalm 29:11 tells us very clearly that, "The Lord gives strength to His people; the Lord blesses His people with peace." "What's going on, God? Why are so many of Your people living so far from the reality of who You are and what You have to offer? I can understand why those who do not know You as savior struggle and walk around defeated, but not those who call You by name. Your Word tells us that it rains on the just and the unjust alike (Matthew 5:45) and the believer is not exempt from trials and tribulations, however, Your Word also encourages Your people to, 'be strong and courageous. Do not be afraid or terrified because of them, for the Lord your God goes with you; He will never leave you nor forsake you.' (Deuteronomy 31:6) What is going on, God?"

He began to speak to my heart, and He showed me the answer to my inquiry was very simple. "Their priorities are all messed up and they would prefer to spend hours in front of the television or on the computer playing senseless games or chatting and blogging over totally insignificant events they have no control over. Anything and everything that holds even the slightest interest seems to be enough to draw them away from a relationship with their Lord. There are so many excuses. Family, friends, jobs, careers, and hobbies all compete with thousands of other issues for their time, however, it filters down to one simple reason. They do not understand My Word. Their Bibles sit on end tables or on bookshelves collecting dust. Instead of relying on My Word they are satisfied with mindless traditions. There are so many who declare that they believe in Me, however, they do not believe Me. I have given them My Word and they refuse to believe it or take advantage of it. It boils down to the fact that they cannot trust Me because they really do not know Me."

My wife and I had the opportunity to help pioneer a church in the small central Illinois town of Pontiac. We did not have a position of responsibility. We simply went to the revival to offer assistance if the team needed help. Several groups from different churches in the surrounding towns had volunteered to help canvass the city and invite those who did not have a church to come to a large revival that was to be held the last weekend of the month. The evangelist was a well-known preacher from Arkansas. Friday night came and a large group of us boarded two Greyhound buses for the forty-minute trip to the auditorium where the meetings were to be held. Minutes before we were to leave, a woman and her young son climbed on board and took a seat across from my wife. No one had a clue who she was or why she had come. They just sat there the entire trip without saying anything. When we arrived, I noticed them enter the building and take seats near the front. The place was packed. There had to be several hundred people there. The music began and the worship and praise were awesome. You could just feel the presence of God. The evangelist began to preach. It was a powerful word of exhortation. Everything was proceeding just like you would have expected when suddenly he stopped preaching, he looked over at the woman and her son, and asked them if they would come up on the stage. Now he did not know this woman. He had never met her before, however, God spoke to him right in the middle of his message. He turned to those in the audience and told them that God had given him a word for this woman that we did not need to hear. He placed the microphone behind his back and proceeded to speak to her. Immediately she began to cry uncontrollably. I honestly thought she was going to collapse. We had no idea what he told her, however, it had a tremendous impact on her.

After the meeting our group boarded the buses for the trip home. The woman and her son once again climbed on board and took a seat. We still did not know who she was or where she came from. A week and a half later during the Sunday morning worship service, a gentleman who we had known for several years, stood up to testify. He had invited the woman and her son to go with him to the meetings. Unfortunately he ran into conflicts at the last minute and could not attend, however, he encouraged them to go anyway. Apparently he had been witnessing to this woman. She had just received word that her son was going to die. He had a rare form of lymphoma that was not responding to chemo or radiation. They had tried bone marrow transplants and nothing seemed to work for long. The doctors had told her that there was nothing more that they could do. They also said she needed to celebrate Christmas early because he would not be here. The meetings were held the last week of August. Time was running out. The gentleman shared how he told her about Jesus and how He could make a difference if only she gave Him a chance. He showed her in I Peter 2:24 where it declared "He bore our sins in His body on the tree, so that we might die to sins and live for righteousness; by His wounds you have been healed." In the midst of her desperation a peace came over her and she said, "I believe that. I will trust my Lord and take my son to the meeting."

The Thursday after the meeting she had to take her son back to the cancer specialist for another evaluation. During the examination an incredulous look came upon the face of the doctor. "The bumps on his neck and chest were gone. This is impossible. I do not understand what is happening. This does not happen. The cancer is gone," he declared. After several other tests the results came back totally normal. There wasn't even a sign that cancer had ever been in his body. Why? Because a desperate mother chose to believe God's Word and give it a chance when things seemed hopeless. God is faithful to His Word. He will respond. "God does not do those things any more," the skeptic scoffs. "Why not?" say I. "His miracles were dispensational. In other words, He needed them to get people's attention so that they would listen to His message." They say. "Hogwash!!"; say I. "Maybe that is exactly why He still does miracles today; to get your attention so that you, oh scoffer, may hear His message."

In the early nineties I had the privilege of ministering with a real character who loved the Lord and loved life. He pastored a small church in Washington Township, Michigan. He was at his desk one afternoon preparing for the upcoming service when he received a phone call from the mother of a young man who had befriended him several months earlier. Unfortunately the young man had suffered a terrible accident. He dove into the shallow end of a swimming pool and broke his neck, leaving him paralyzed from the neck down. He had asked his mother to call and see if Pastor would have time to come and talk to him. His future was uncertain and, at best, he faced a life of total dependency on others for his every need. To say the least, he was desperate.

"Pastor, do you think this Jesus you have been telling me about can do something for me?"

"Young man, it is not important what I believe. Do you believe He can?"

"I am not sure, Pastor. I would like to believe He could."

The pastor began to walk the young man through the Gospels and show him how Jesus made a difference in the lives of so many whose situations seemed hopeless. He gave sight to the blind, healed the lame, cured the lepers, and even raised people from the dead.

"What makes you doubt whether He can do it for you?

"He can, Pastor. I really believe that Jesus can heal me also."

"Are you saying that just to gain His favor for a season?"

"What are you talking about, Pastor?"

"If Jesus would heal you, would you continue to love Him and serve Him?"

"Yes, Pastor, I would serve Him for the rest of my life. I know that I would."

"Young man, that is easy to say when you are in the condition you are in. What if He chose not to heal you. Will you still love Him the rest of your life? Will you still serve Him? Will you still trust Him to meet all your needs?"

After a pause that seemed to last an eternity, the young man began to cry and with tears streaming down his cheeks he declared, "Lord, whether You heal me or not, I am going to trust You, and I promise that I will serve You the rest of my life no matter how long that may be." Immediately feeling began to creep into his fingers and his toes. He began to move his fingers and then his hands and then his arms. Within minutes he was standing and walking to the amazement of his mother. Unexplainable joy and excitement filled that house that day as Jesus totally restored that young man. It wasn't about the pastor or what he believed. It was all about a young man who came to a point in his life where he was willing to totally believe God and trust Him even in the midst of his impossible situation. He heard God's Word. He believed it was for him and God showed Himself to be faithful.

This is so important, to understand that God is simply waiting for us to believe what He says in His Word is true – we can claim his promises. We can trust Him!

These are real accounts of real people with extraordinary needs, probably very similar to the situations many of you find yourselves in. None of these individuals had a special dispensation of grace. They are just like you and me. They are common people who needed an uncommon touch from an awesome, loving, merciful God who simply waited until they came to the point where they not only believed in Him, but they came to the point where they believed what He promised was true.

I know of what I speak because my wife and I experienced firsthand God's grace and faithfulness. It was only a couple of months after the bankruptcy. I had worked hard and saved enough money to take my family to Grandma and Grandpa's for an extended weekend. It was difficult because we were living from paycheck to paycheck. Things were slowly beginning to settle down and come together, however, we were still not able to save anything.

The boys absolutely loved their grandparents and were excited about going. It was a five-hour trip that was relatively uneventful except for an unscheduled stop to apply the "board of education to the seat of learning" to three boys who would not leave their hands off each other. For those who have experienced the joys of traveling with a 10-year-old, an 8-year-old, and a 4-year-old, you know what I am talking about. We arrived in Des Moines, Iowa, in the late afternoon. However, before we could go to my in-laws' house, I had to stop at Target to get some motor oil. Our car, even though it wasn't the best, performed very well on the trip, however, we had to baby it. It had a tendency to burn oil and I knew that a trip that long would require a refill. When I came to the checkout counter to pay, the unimaginable happened. I did not have my billfold.

What in the world could have happened to it? We went back out to the car and looked all around in the car and the parking lot – nothing. We went back inside and asked the manager if he would keep an eye out for it. We called the gas station we refueled at in What Cheer, Iowa. Nothing! No one had seen my billfold. Every cent we had to our name was in that billfold, including my driver's license and credit cards. Now what? BC it would have been panic city, however, there was a strange sense of peace that came over both my wife and me. When we reached the folks' house, we explained what happened, and then we did something that surprised her parents. We gathered together as a family, knelt down on the floor, and told the Lord that we were going to completely trust Him with our circumstances and needs. The only thing we asked was that He let the billfold be found by someone who really needed it. Please do not let a druggie or an alcoholic find it. We proceeded to have a great time with the folks, however, all good things must come to an end. As we prepared to leave for home, my in-laws made sure that we had enough money to get home and buy groceries for the week. That was a huge sacrifice for them because they were not very well off.

A couple of weeks after our trip we received a call from my father in law. My in-laws had a very dear friend whom they had known most of their lives. She was an 82-year-old widow who lived alone and found great pleasure in reading the Des Moines Sunday Register from cover to cover. The paper is huge, not because of the amount of news, but because of the thousands upon thousands of two- and three-line ads that filled the want ads section. As she was faithfully searching through the ads, she noticed something that caught her attention. The ad was for a refrigerator that a gentleman was selling. That was of no interest to her; however, the last part of the ad said that a billfold had been found in the Target parking lot. Could this be the billfold that my father-in-law had told her about? She called my wife's parents who in turn called the number in the ad. Sure enough he had my billfold. When my father-in-law went to pick it up, he was amazed to see that everything was still intact. There was nothing missing. The gentleman even refused to take a reward. God is faithful. He is true to His Word. We did not really expect to see it again. We had not prayed for its return. We simply said give it to someone who really needed it and He did. He gave it back to us. What a blessing. We could have gotten all upset and we could have allowed our emotions to ruin our trip; however, we refused to let that happen. We made a decision to trust God for our needs.

I guess what it boils down to is this. When the world deals you a lemon, what are you going to do with it? You choose. You decide what your circumstances and situations will become. We all have them. You will never be able to escape from them or shelter yourself from them. You are going to experience times in your life where you are going to be tested, tried, and stretched. Why would you be so foolish or naïve to think that you can escape them when Jesus could not. His circumstances led Him to the point where He was crucified on the cross and yet at no time do we hear Him complaining or throwing a pity party. He simply trusted His Father to walk Him through them. Have you read or studied the Word of God enough to know and understand what is available to you as a believer? Have you seen in the Word where it declares that, "Even though I walk through the valley of the shadow of death, I will fear no evil, for You are with me; Your rod and Your staff, they comfort me" (Psalm 23:4).

My wife and I are personally aware of many testimonies from people who have come to the point in their lives where they made a commitment to simply trust the Lord in the midst of their trying and potentially serious situations.

There was a young man in his late twenties who had been coming to church for some time. To look at him you would think that he was "messed up". Much of his potential had been wasted on alcohol and drugs. It was very difficult for him to carry on a conversation. His mind would wander and in the middle of a sentence he would forget what he was talking about. The alcohol and drugs had robbed him of his ability to function in a normal way. He could not hold a job and had to live with his parents who were on the verge of having him institutionalized. There did not seem to be too much hope for him. Once a month a group would come together with Pastor on a Friday evening and spend the entire night in prayer and reading the Word of God. The next morning everyone would go out to breakfast before heading home. Now this was not an exercise to prove how holy we were. The time was spent interceding for a "Healing and Deliverance" service that was held the last Sunday evening of each month. It just so happened that this young man showed up for one of the services. The pastor preached a challenging message on faith and God's desire to make a difference in our lives if we would simply trust Him with our impossibilities. During the altar call the young man made his way to the front and stood in line with those who were seeking help from the Lord. When the pastor finally came to him, the young man told him that he hated his life. He did not want to continue living the way he was. He was frightened and frustrated and confused.

"Do you believe that Jesus can make a difference in your life?"

"Yes, I do, Pastor."

"Do you believe that He wants to make a difference in your life?"

"Yes, I do, Pastor."

"Then tell Him that, and tell Him you are going to trust Him and give Him a chance."

Immediately the Holy Spirit laid the young man on his back. The shaking that accompanied him wherever he went ceased. A calm came over him and a sense of peace flooded the front. I do not know how long he remained on the floor, however, I do know that Pastor ministered to the rest of those who wanted prayer and most of the people had left for home. When he did stand up, it was apparent that a tremendous change had occurred. He was vibrant, excited, full of joy, and literally unable to contain his enthusiasm for what Jesus had done for him. His parents were amazed. It was the son they knew years earlier before he became involved with drinking and drugs. He was totally delivered from his dependencies. For the first time in years he was able to carry on an intelligent conversation. It was not long after that a young woman entered his life. Today they are happily married and the parents of three great children. He has a very good job and a bright future. Once again we ask the question: why? And once again we arrive at the same answer. The young man in his desperation chose to believe God and trust Him when all else seemed hopeless.

Every New Year's Eve, for several years, we would hold a special service at the church. A southern gospel group known as the Goodman Family from Florida would come and put on a concert. The same evangelist who spoke at the Pontiac, Illinois, meetings would come and minister to us. In one particular meeting a mother and her son were sitting in the front row across from the choir. The service was great. The singing was inspiring. The congregation was ready for a challenging message when the evangelist stopped and came down from the podium and went to where the mother and her son were sitting. He had never met this family and knew nothing of their situation. He simply did what the Holy Spirit had told him to do and went to the boy, pointed his finger at him, and said, "In the name of Jesus be healed." For the first time in his six years the child turned to his mother and said, "Mommy". What a thrill it was for the mother to hear her son speak. He had been born deaf. He could not speak. He had never spoken and yet that night God answered a mother's prayer and restored her son to perfect health. For years she had been asking and begging God to do something for her son. Suddenly scriptures she had read before began to leap off the pages. Her heart was stirred when she saw Matthew 15:30,31.

"Great crowds came to Him, bringing the lame, the blind, the crippled, the mute and many others, and laid them at His feet; and He healed them. The people were amazed when they saw the mute speaking, the crippled made well, the lame walking, and the blind seeing. And they praised the God of Israel."

If He could do it then, He could do it now for her son. "Lord, I am going to stop begging You. I am going to lay my son at Your feet and believe that You can help him. I am going to begin trusting in Your Word." Within days of making that declaration, God heard, God responded, and her son was totally healed.

This is the reality of living for and trusting in the Lord Jesus Christ. Hebrews 13:8 declares, "Jesus Christ is the same yesterday and today and forever." He has not changed. He will not change. He cannot change. It is an integral part of His deity. He is immutable, which simply means unchanging. Those who trusted Him 2,000 years ago received what they were searching for. Those who trusted Him 500 years ago received what they were searching for. Those you have met in these pages trusted Him and received what they were searching for. He will do the same for you today. Do not limit what He can do for you by doubt or unbelief. If there is no room in your traditions for the miracle working reality of a mighty, awesome, compassionate Savior, then maybe it is time to revisit your traditions and ask why. Is it time to simply say, "enough is enough," and begin to let the Word of God speak to your heart? Is it time to stop simply "believing in" and time to start "believing" what He says?

> "But let all who take refuge (trust) in You be glad; let them ever sing for joy. Spread Your protection over them, that those who love Your name may rejoice in You. For surely, O Lord, You bless the righteous; You surround them with Your favor as with a shield" Psalm 5:11,12.

It is very easy to get discouraged, frustrated and pessimistic, especially with all the devastation, economic peril, warfare, perversion, temptation, humanistic reasoning, and loose living all around us. However, for those who have learned to believe the Word of God, trust the Word of God, and give it a chance, it is a great time to be alive, especially if you truly know that

God Loves the Common Person

I Want All of You, Lord

The last thing I expected, at least from my new Christian friends, was confusion, however, that is exactly what I found. It was only a couple of months after I asked Jesus into my life when I found myself faced with a situation I did not know how to handle. Needless to say, I was not one to keep quiet. I could not help but testify of the changes the Lord made in my life. I would tell anyone who would listen. Naturally I ran into a large amount of skepticism, a fair share of ridicule, and a heavy dose of rejection. However, that did not surprise me considering how I treated people BC. The one thing I was not prepared for were all the well-meaning religious people who gave me advice. You know, "You have to do it this way," "you have to do it that way," and "be careful who you listen to or what you believe" kind of advice that simple created a sense of confusion. For instance, a very serious believer emphatically told me to be careful of all those tongues talkers who will lead me astray. Tongues talking is of the devil and will lead me straight to hell. Wouldn't you know it, not more than a couple of days later I was in a conversation with one of those tongues talkers who insisted I was not completely saved until I talked in tongues.

Now wait just a minute. Both of them could not be right. Matter of fact, I doubted if either of them was near the truth because they could not show me in the Word where they came up with their theologies. I know I was young in the Lord and there were many things I needed to learn about my relationship with Jesus and what He expected of me, however, I knew that confusion was not part of the package. God is too big and awesome and wise to be confused. The truth had to lie somewhere in the middle of those two extremes. I guess it was time for some serious "rug time". "Lord, I know You are not the God of confusion. I do not know what to believe. I guess I am simply going to trust You to reveal the truth to me. All I know is I want all of You. I am not satisfied with just part of You. I am open to what ever You might have for me."

That evening was like any other evening. After supper my wife and I spent time with the boys doing our usual wrestling and roughhousing. It seemed like the kids were bound and determined to gang up on Dad and get him on the floor. It was several years and many pounds later, however, before they were able to accomplish that. You would have thought they won the Olympics when they finally succeeded. Nine o'clock came and it was time for the boys to hit the sacks. You know how kids can be. It took a little gentle persuasion from mom to convince them. My wife and I climbed into bed and she snuggled up to me like she usually did for our time of prayer before calling it quits for the day. It was at that point when all sense of normalcy vanished. As I was lying there, I could sense what felt like a huge pressure on the inside that wanted to explode out of me. As I started to talk to the Lord, the most awesome heavenly language began to flow out of me. I felt like I was floating three feet above the bed. Tears of joy and excitement flowed down my cheeks. My wife responded exactly how I would have expected her to. She freaked out. She was convinced that I had finally gone off the deep end. I could not help but laugh when I looked and saw her peeking around the bedroom door. Her mouth was wide open and her eyes were as big as quarters. She would not come near me. I do not know how long it was before I came to the point where I could explain to her what I had told the Lord. I know it was some time. Even after the explanation, she made sure there was maximum distance between us when she did return to bed. I guess I could not blame her because I knew what happened, but I did not have a clue how to describe it to her so she would understand.

    The next morning during my time with the Lord, I was quick to thank Him for His awesome gift; however, the one thing I needed for Him to show me was the truth of what I experienced in a way that both my wife and I could understand. Wouldn't you know it, the very next time I opened the Bible to read,

I turned to the eighth chapter of John and saw these words. "If you continue in My Word, then are you My disciples indeed; and you shall know the truth, and the truth shall make you free" (John 8:31,32). From there I proceeded to read everything I could find in the Word concerning what I had experienced. Of course I visited such well-known accounts as the second chapter of Acts. I went with Peter as he was sent to Cornelius' house in the tenth chapter of Acts. I also read Paul's teaching on the gifts of the Spirit in I Corinthians chapters 11 and 12. However, I still did not understand what took place in a way that I could explain it to my wife. It was about this time that our pastor began a series on what he called the typology of the Old Testament. He took us to Hebrews and showed us where the author declares that the Law, or the Old Testament, was a picture or a type of the "good things to come". Every doctrine revealed in the New Testament is hidden in and protected by the types and shadows of the Old Testament. Now this sounded like something I could get into. We journeyed into the Wilderness and visited the nation of Israel as they were encamped around the Tabernacle in Exodus, Leviticus, and Numbers. For those who are not familiar with the Old Testament or the Tabernacle, let it suffice to say that the Tabernacle was the place where God chose to take up residency among His people on earth. He had given Moses very detailed instructions on how to build the Tabernacle itself, the furniture that was to be placed in the Tabernacle, and the ceremonies associated with it.

> "Then have them make a sanctuary for Me, and I will dwell among them. Make this tabernacle and all its furnishings exactly like the pattern I will show you." Exodus 25:8,9

Every detail in its construction and function was, in some way, a picture of the person, character, and ministry of Jesus either here on earth or in heaven. Also hidden within the details of the Tabernacle are pictures of God's plan for the redemption of mankind and our place and responsibilities as born-again believers. Things were getting very interesting. Now I was getting somewhere. All I had to do was locate the picture that explained what had happened that night. How was I going to accomplish that? I had not gone to Bible college yet. I definitely was not a well-versed Bible scholar. This was going to be a daunting task. However, I was amazed at how the Word came alive as I read and reread the accounts of the Tabernacle in the Wilderness. Remember what I saw in John 8:31,32? The Word of God is true. It works!

It seemed like every time I began to study the Tabernacle, I would get to the account of the Golden

Lampstand and that is where I would stop. The Lampstand was located in the Holy Place in front of the Veil. The Holy Place was the first of two rooms in the Tabernacle proper. The Holy Place was separated from the Holy of Holies by a large veil. The only piece of furniture in the Holy of Holies was the Golden Ark of the Covenant. God told Moses that He would take up residency in the Nation of Israel on the Mercy Seat which was the lid that covered the Ark. The High Priest was the only one allowed to enter the Holy of Holies, and then only once a year on the Day of Atonement during the Passover Feast. There were three pieces of furniture in the Holy Place including the Golden Altar of Incense on which incense was burned; the Table of Shewbread upon which sat twelve loaves of bread, one for each of the twelve tribes; and the Golden Lampstand which was to burn continually.

Now stay with me and let's see if we can recognize the picture I was looking for. The Golden Lampstand was hammered out of a solid piece of gold. It was not made from a pattern which could be used to make gold castings. It was unique. It could not be reproduced. It was a beaten work. Isaiah 53:5 declares, "But He was wounded for our transgressions, He was bruised for our iniquities: the chastisement of our peace was upon Him; and with His stripes we are healed." Jesus was a beaten work.

There were seven branches on the Lampstand, and each branch held a flowerlike cup shaped like an almond bud. The cups were filled with the purest and finest olive oil that could be made. "Command the Israelites to bring you clear oil of pressed olives for the light so that the lamps may be kept burning continually" (Leviticus 24:2). The priest would then take a wick that he had woven out of flax and place it into the oil. The coarse flax would then become soft and pliable as the oil began to saturate it. The priest would then light the wick and the oil would burn, giving off light. Now everything in the tabernacle made of gold represented some aspect of the Lord Jesus. Everything that was not gold was a picture of some aspect of the believer and his relationship with the Lord. Hey! That's it! I am the wick. "Hey, God, that is awesome," said I. "Hold on now. I am not quite finished," said He. From there the Holy Spirit began to reveal how what was hidden in the Old Testament was revealed in the New Testament. John the Baptist in Luke 3:16 declared "I baptize you with water. But one more powerful than I will come, the thongs of whose sandals I am not worthy to untie. He will baptize you with the Holy Spirit and fire."

Finally I understood. It was not a matter of having to choose between man's theologies. It was a simple matter of desiring all that God had for me and trusting that He would honor that desire. It is not complicated. God is not a God of confusion. Follow with me the process that takes place when an individual accepts Christ Jesus as Lord and Savior.

> "Therefore, if anyone is in Christ, he is a new creation; the old has gone, the new has come!" II Corinthians 5:17

> "Do you not know that your body is a temple of the Holy Spirit, who is in you, whom you have received from God? You are not your own; you were bought at a price. Therefore honor God with your body." I Corinthians 6:19,20

If you have accepted Jesus as Lord and Savior, you have the Holy Spirit living inside of you. You do not have to wait or tarry for Him to fall. The disciples who were together on the Day of Pentecost were told to go and wait until the power came from on high. That is totally understandable if you realize that the Holy Spirit could not come to the believers until Jesus' earthly ministry was completed, the resurrection had taken place, and Jesus ascended into heaven. On the Day of Pentecost the Holy Spirit took up residence in His Temple and He has not left. He fell 2,000 years ago. He does not have to fall again.

In order to bring the picture of the wick to life in our lives, all we have to do is exactly what the wick had to do. It had to yield and become pliable so that the oil could flow through it. In other words, we have to humble ourselves, surrender our wills for His will, and yield to the flow of the "oil" within us. Then our High Priest, the Lord Jesus Christ, can light the wick and our fire will burn just as He did for the disciples on the Day of Pentecost.

> "When the day of Pentecost came, they were all together in one place. Suddenly a sound like the blowing of a violent wind came from heaven and filled the whole house where they were sitting. They saw what seemed to be tongues of fire that separated and came to rest on each of them. All of them were filled with the Holy Spirit and began to speak in other tongues as the Spirit enabled them." Acts 2:1-4

Whether you can accept the idea of a heavenly language or not because of your traditions or theologies does not change the fact that God honored His Word and gave me all of Him just as I asked. Matter of fact, when I explained what the Lord had revealed to me to my family in a way they could understand, they also began to hunger for all of God. It was not long after that when Charles and

Francis Hunter came to town. There must have been 2,000-plus people at their meeting. During the service Francis indicated that there would be an opportunity for those who wanted to experience the release of the Holy Spirit after the meeting was over. My wife could not wait. As soon as the people were dismissed, she followed Francis to the other side of the building. To my amazement seven hundred others went with her. It did not take long until the most beautiful harmony I had ever heard filled that place. You could absolutely feel the presence of the Holy Spirit as seven hundred believers began to worship and sing in an incredible blend of heavenly languages. What a truly remarkable experience that was. When my wife returned, she was so full of joy and peace she could hardly speak. All she wanted to do was praise her Lord in her new language.

Now I cannot finish this section without giving you the same caution the Lord gave me. There has been far too much division and discord within the Body of Christ over the issue of speaking in tongues. What a tragedy because it is not about tongues. It is about the release of the Holy Spirit in the believer's life. The heavenly language is simply a sign that verifies the fact that something special occurred on the inside. It is a tool that God has given us to help us in our relationship with Jesus.

"In the same way, the Spirit helps us in our weakness. We do not know what we ought to pray for, but the Spirit Himself intercedes for us with groans that words cannot express. And He who searches our hearts knows the mind of the Spirit, because the Spirit intercedes for the saints in accordance with God's will." Romans 6:26,27

Speaking in a heavenly language is not a prerequisite for salvation. You do not need to speak in tongues in order to be saved, nor will you go to hell if you do. Salvation is totally dependent upon believing and confessing.

"But what does it say? The Word is near you; it is in your mouth and in your heart, that is, the word of faith we are proclaiming: That if you confess with your mouth, Jesus is Lord, and believe in your heart that God raised Him from the dead, you will be saved. For it is with your heart that you believe and are justified, and it is with your mouth that you confess and are saved."

The only issue the believer who rejects the idea of a heavenly language may deal with is falling short of or not having the ability to achieve all that God has called him or her to do. I, for one, am incredibly thankful to a merciful and gracious God who knows my weaknesses and has provided a helper for me when times are tough or my emotions raise their ugly head and get in the way. Many times, when the battle was raging and I either did not know what to pray for or was not in a proper frame of mind to pray as I should, I would simply call upon the Holy Spirit living inside of me to intercede on my behalf. The amazing truth is, when I rely on and trust in Him, no matter what I might be going through, He has never let me down or failed me. He does not always allow me to do or say what I want to. He may even have to slap my hand and correct me; however, I know that His precious gift of the Holy Spirit living in me will help me return to and stay on the path that the Father has set before me. Why? Because I know that I know

God Loves the Common Person

Lord, I Want My Family to Know You

We had just settled down for the night. The kids were finally in bed. My wife and I were reviewing what had taken place earlier in the day and what we were going to do the next afternoon after church when the phone rang. Now I don't know about you, however, when the phone rings at unwelcome times my first thought is "Now what happened?"

"Terry!"

"Hi, Mom. What's wrong? Has something happened to Dad?"

"No. It is not your dad. Grandma has taken a turn for the worse and, if you want to see her again, you might want to come up as soon as you can."

"Okay, Mom. Linda and I will be up there in the morning."

Needless to say I had a difficult time sleeping that night. I loved my grandma even though she was a real character. She was 4' 11", 98 pounds soaking wet, and a formidable figure. Not much happened around her house without her knowing it or approving of it. She definitely had a domineering personality. Now Grandpa was just the opposite. He was a very docile and timid individual who took life in stride and never seemed to let anything bother him. One thing he was very good at, however, was getting both of us in trouble. "Okay, little one, let's go get dirty," he would whisper with a little chuckle, and off we would go to the coal bin. "I bet I can put more coal in the hopper than you can," he would declare and the race was on. I must have either been a great coal slinger or Grandpa was a great hustler, because I always beat him and it did not seem like he did too much. It was a lot of fun, but afterward, we knew what was going to happen.

"What in heaven's name do you think you are doing letting a child like him go into that filthy place? Are you out of your mind? Now both of you up to the tub and do not come down until you are as clean as a baby's hind end or I will take this skillet to your head."

I remember asking Gramps why we couldn't pretend to take a bath and go back down all dirty and see what Grandma would really do. "Whoa now, you do not want to tempt fate. You have a lot of living yet to do," was his reply. That was good enough for me. I loved to go to Grandma's and Grandpa's house. There were all kinds of neat places to hide from the sheriff's posse. One day I found a door inside their closet that led to the closet in the next room. What was I doing in their closet? Why does a six- or seven-year-old kid do anything? I do not have a clue, however, what a great escape route when you are running from pirates or playing hide and seek with your siblings. In their living room sat an old elliptical-shaped table with a cloth that hung clear down to the floor. That was another cool hiding place. Grandma would always hide these little round toasty things behind the cereal. I believe they were called Holland Rusks. I am not sure if they are made any more, however, I sure loved them and every once in a while a nasty outlaw would heist one and run and hide under the table. Looking back, I really do not think I got by with too much, however, I loved it. Then one day everything changed. My mom was taking me to school when she told me that Grandpa had a heart attack and did not make it. To an eight-year-old, that was crushing news and all I could do was cry. I was so devastated I could not stay in school. It was not the same after that. Grandma sold the old home and moved into an apartment. From there she went into a senior's center and eventually into a very large senior care facility run by the Moose. As the years passed, however, I never lost my love for my grandma, and my wife and children and I would visit her as often as we could.

We made arrangements with good friends who said they would take the boys to church and watch them until we returned. It was a two-hour-trip from home to where she was. When we arrived, neither my wife nor I was prepared for what we saw. Grandma looked terrible. I did not even recognize her. She was all swollen and had awful looking bedsores all over her body. It simply broke my heart to see her like that. I had an ache in the pit of my stomach all the way home. The first thing I did when we returned was call Pastor Phil. We were young in the Lord and I did not yet understand the authority we have in Jesus. I thought maybe he could help and go with me to give Grandma communion and pray for her.

Pastor quickly agreed and let me know that he would be pleased to. He is a neat guy. The Holy Spirit was really working in his life. You might say that he was living outside of the box when it came to the beliefs of his denomination. He truly loved the Lord and walked in a freedom of the Spirit that drew me to him. We left early the next morning, and when we walked into the facility where Grandma was, we heard a country western band playing in the dining room. We made our way down the hall and into her room. We could still hear the band; however, it did not interfere with what we were there for. Grandma looked so helpless and uncomfortable. She was so weak she could hardly speak. I let her know that she did not have to say anything. We simply wanted to make sure she had an opportunity to take communion and then we wanted to pray for her. "Is that okay, Grandma?" With a little glint in her eyes, a smile on her face, and a nod of the head, she let us know that she liked that idea. Pastor took out his little ministry book and opened it to the communion service. As soon as he opened the book, the band stopped playing right in the middle of a country western song and began to play "How Great Thou Art." "Wow, do you hear that," said I. "I sure do", said he, and he proceeded to minister communion. She was so weak she could not swallow the wafer. I had to take it out of her mouth. My heart ached. With tears in my eyes, I turned to Pastor and asked him if he believed that Jesus could heal her or at least give her a perfect peace until He came for her.

"Terry, I believe that He is able to do whatever we ask if we ask in faith. Do you believe that He can?" he asked me.

"Yes, I do, Pastor. I believe that He loves my grandma and will give me the desire of my heart. I do not want her to suffer like she is any more."

"That is all He needs to hear. Now you pray for your grandma and I will agree with you."

"Father God, I know You love my grandma even more than I do. If it breaks my heart to see her like this, then I have to believe it also breaks Yours. There is nothing in me that can make a difference in her except You. You can, and I believe You want to. In Jesus' name I ask you to heal her, however, if it is her time to go home, at least give her perfect peace until the Lord comes for her."

There was such a peace and joy that filled that room. It is difficult to really adequately explain it. All I know is that Pastor and I left singing and rejoicing in our Lord. Praying for Grandma was the easy part. Now came the difficult task. I had to let my parents know what we had done. We drove into their driveway only to see that they were gone. That bothered me because I knew the Lord had told me to let my mom know; however, they were not there. So we decided to leave and I would call them as soon as I got home. We pulled out of the driveway and my folks turned into the driveway. Perfect timing! Coincidence? No way. We got out of the car and I introduced Pastor to my folks. I then told Mom to be prepared for a miracle and explained to her what we had done. That is when all sense of normalcy disappeared. She proceeded to unload on us. We had a lot of nerve doing something like that. Grandma did not need a couple of religious fanatics giving her false hope. She then entered into a five-minute tirade that literally blew Pastor away. I pretty well knew what to expect, but that poor guy was totally caught off guard. I failed to inform him what kind of woman my mom was. When I was finally able to get a word in, I told her that I loved her and we left. We had a great trip home. Mom's temper tantrum did not dampen our excitement. We knew that something special was going to happen and believed it would be a testimony to my parents. The following Sunday the phone rang and once again it was Mom.

"Terry, you are going to have to come up here. You will not believe Grandma. She is giving the helpers and the nurses all kinds of trouble. She won't let them feed her or bathe her. She is being a real stinker. She wants to see you and Linda. I do not understand what is happening."

"Okay, Mom. We are on our way.

With a sense of excitement, I loaded the family into the car and off we went. I did not know what to expect however, I knew it would be good. When we got there my parents had just left to get something to eat. We went into Grandma's room and she jumped up from her chair and gave us all a hug. She was the woman I knew twenty-five years earlier. God had completely restored her. No more bedsores. She was vibrant and full of life. The aides could not believe what had happened. They were convinced she was going to die. We had a great time with her. When we finally did catch up with my parents, I tried to explain to Mom what I believed happened, and she did not want anything to do with it.

"I am not interested in any of that religious stuff. Grandma is a strong woman and she just got better. The doctors did a great job with her."

"Okay, Mom. If that is what you want to believe, it is okay."

I did not want to cause a problem. I know if I had continued, she would have lost her temper. So home we went rejoicing in the Lord and giving thanks for a great miracle. Six months later, almost to the day, the phone rang once again.

"Terry, Grandma was taken to the hospital. She is not doing well at all. Can you come up?"

"Yes, Mom. Linda and I are on our way."

When we reached the hospital and walked into Grandma's room, we knew that today was her day to go to be with the Lord. It was a good day. It was not something to grieve over. She knew the Lord as her Savior. It was a time to celebrate. God had been faithful and had given her six months of perfect health and perfect peace, just like Pastor Phil and I had asked for. It was obvious, however, that Mom was having problems with the situation. I finally convinced her that she needed to go home and get some rest because she had been up all night and had not eaten. My aunt was flying in from California and she needed to be there when she arrived. Once we were alone I sat down next to Grandma and began reading the Gospel of John to her. My wife sat down in a chair at her feet and began to pray quietly. To look at her, you would have thought she could not hear you. She was in a coma, however, when I came to her favorite Scripture and began to read it, a little smile appeared on her face. "For God so loved the world that He gave His one and only Son, that whoever believes in Him shall not perish but have eternal life" (John 3:16). I am not sure how long we sat there. I read a considerable portion of Scripture to her and had been telling her what she had to look forward to. I had just informed her how much we were going to miss her when the temperature in the room shot up dramatically. It got warm. My wife and I knew that the presence of God was there. Grandma's breathing changed. She relaxed and simply walked into glory with her Lord. What an experience. Linda let out a yell and then caught herself. She came over next to me and we laid hands on what was left of Grandma and gave thanks for the extra time we had with her and thanked Him for His mercy and grace toward her. It was just a matter of minutes after the nurses and the doctor had come in and verified the fact that she was dead when Mom and my aunt walked in. Needless to say, Mom went hysterical and blamed herself for what happened because she was not there. It was a difficult time for her. She would not listen to anything Linda and I had to say. I am thankful that my aunt and uncle were believers. They understood when we shared with them what happened and had a great peace about everything. It would have been nice if they could have been there to bid her good-bye, however, they knew they would see her again someday. She assured me that she knew how to handle Mom and everything would be okay.

"You did what you needed to do, Terry, and we both appreciate it very much. It will be a while before your mom settles down. Uncle Frank and I will take care of everything. There is a lot we have to do so you and Linda go on home and we will see you again in a few days."

All the way home I carried such a great burden for my mom and dad. I wanted so much to have a meaningful relationship with them. It had been very difficult growing up not only for me, but for my brother and two sisters also. As a family we were totally dysfunctional. Every other day seemed to be World War III. There was little peace and no love. At least nothing that I could relate to what I thought love should be. About that time my wife and I became involved with a program called Lay Witness Missions. It was an organization that would send teams of twenty to twenty-four people into the mainstream liturgical churches and hold weekend retreats. There was such a church in the little town of Fenton, Illinois. It was located approximately forty miles from where my folks lived. The church had just completed a building project and for the first time in their history the generational barriers were down. The young and the old worked side-by-side to see the building built, and they did not want to lose that camaraderie; therefore a Lay Witness Mission's team was invited to help them understand what needed to happen next. It was a great weekend and we saw many great healings and many walls come down between children and parents and young and old. It was powerful. Usually after the concluding service on Sunday morning, there would be a going away potluck. This particular meal I knew my wife and I were going to miss. I felt compelled to call Mom and Dad and ask them if they would join us for lunch at a popular buffet in Rock Island, Illinois, called Sir George's which they surprisingly agreed to do. When we arrived the place was crowded, however, we were able to get a table without too much waiting. We had a great meal and talked about rather insignificant happenings. When we finished and were about to leave, my dad and I stood up and I asked him if he would sit down for a minute. I had something I wanted to say.

"Mom and Dad, Linda and I love you very much. I am not sure if you will understand what I am saying, however, we claim you in the name of the Lord Jesus Christ. I do not know what it is going to take for you to accept Jesus as your Savior, however, you are not going anywhere until you do. If it comes to the point where you get tired of living, all you have to do is ask Jesus into your life and you can go home anytime you want."

I did not have a clue what to expect. You do not talk to my dad like that, but what happened caught my wife and me off guard. He started to cry. In my 31 years I had never seen my dad cry. My mom started to cry. Needless to say Linda and I both began to cry. Afterward we gave each other hugs in the parking lot and said our good-byes. There was an eerie silence in the car as we started home. I could not believe that I had the boldness to say what I did. It absolutely had to be a God thing. As we turned onto Interstate 74 heading south toward home, the most incredible singing I ever heard filled the car. I glanced down at the tape player in the dash and asked my wife if she had put a worship tape on that I had not heard before. She assured me she had not, and she said she did not hear anything. I heard the angels in heaven singing and it was a witness to me that God was going to honor our boldness. I knew that I knew that there would come a day when both Mom and Dad would know Jesus as their Savior. What I did not know is that it would take many years for my dad and even longer for Mom.

It was in September of 1993 when I received a phone call from Mom informing me that the doctors had told her that Dad had only days left to live. The pancreatic cancer that was eating him alive was getting worse. Without hesitation I informed my employer that I was going to take a week of vacation and spend it with him.

I wanted so bad to talk to him alone and for some reason it did not work out until early Thursday afternoon. Dad was sitting in his chair by the window, and I could tell that he was very uncomfortable. I asked him if he wanted to lie down and rest, and he said he did. I helped him up and to his bed. After making him comfortable and tucking him in, I leaned over and asked him if he remembered the conversation we had in the restaurant 18 years earlier. For the second time in my life I saw tears flowing down his cheek as he shook his head yes.

"Dad, you are very tired, aren't you?"

"Yes, I am," he replied in a weak voice.

"You are ready to go home, aren't you?"

"Yes."

"Have you made your peace with Jesus?"

"Yes, I have," he declared.

My father accepted Jesus as his Lord and Savior that afternoon. Eighteen years. Why did it take so long? I do not have a clue, however, that is not the important thing. What really mattered was he knew Jesus. After hugging him and giving him a kiss on the cheek, I told him that I loved him, and I assured him that he could go home anytime he wanted to. He closed his eyes and never woke up again. Saturday came and he was still with us. I knew why. My brother had not yet arrived, and he was not ready to go until he knew Denny was there. It must have been around one o'clock in the afternoon when I heard the door open and my brother announce that he had finally arrived. He quickly made his way to the side of the bed and said, "Dad, I am here. It is me, Dennis." We reached down and cradled Dad in our arms. We wanted to move him so that he would be more comfortable. As we held him, he gasped his last breath and went home to be with his Lord. For the rest of the family it was a trying time, especially Mom. However, I knew that there would come a day when I would see him again. What a tremendous joy filled my soul.

Mom, on the other hand, proved to be more of a challenge. She insisted on living by herself which put a burden on my youngest sister. Sue lived closest to Mom and yet she was still 3 ½ hours away in Quincy, Illinois. There were many times when she was forced to go and stay with Mom for up to a week at a time. I admire my sister for her willingness to invest the time and effort. It had to be difficult. Mom was not an easy woman to be around. That continued for several years until she received a phone call informing her that Mom had been in a car accident and was in the hospital. She was turning into a shopping center and evidently had a series of minor strokes. She was unaware of a car coming toward her and she turned right in front of him. Fortunately she was still alive. Unfortunately she had broken her wrists and could not go home unless someone was there to take care of her. I did not know it at the time, but my sisters had made the decision to take her to Quincy and place her in a nursing home. When I found out, I knew that I could not let that happen. As problematic and troublesome as she was, she was still Mom and I felt an obligation to do as much as I could to help her. My wife and

I had agreed that she needed to come and live with us. The next day we made arrangements to go and move her back to Michigan. We rented a U-Haul truck and took off. It was an eight-hour trip. Going there was not a problem, however, by the time we returned home we had some serious reservations about our decision.

Needless to say, Mom was Mom, and she had not changed much. We both knew that we had some real challenges ahead of us; however, we also knew that it was something we had to do. She ended up living with us for two years, and during those two years we came to the realization that she redefined the definition of vanity. What a challenge, especially for my wife who had never experienced anyone like her. I honestly believe my wife should be considered for sainthood. It is easy to look back on those years and breathe a sigh of relief that they are over; and yet at the same time, we can point to several defining moments where we knew that the Lord was working in her. The only thing we required of her when she moved in with us was she had to go to church with us. At first the idea met with great resistance, however, we held our ground and she went. She came to the point where she actually enjoyed going because she met several women her own age who simply overlooked her flaws and accepted her for who she was. That was totally new to her. There even came times when I would catch her looking around at those who had their hands raised while they were worshipping.

I asked her one day, "Mom do you know why they are raising their hands?"

"No, Why? It does not make sense to me."

"They love Jesus and are simply doing what the Word of God tells them to do."

"What do you mean, the Word tells them?"

"The Word of God tells us to lift holy hands unto the Lord."

It was not long after that I saw her quickly slip her hands up. She would not leave them up long nor would she lift them all the way, however, she did sneak them up part way. It was comical and it was difficult for me to keep from laughing. My wife and I could see the hardness and stiffness that defined her life slowly disappear. It was time. I asked her if she was ready to accept Jesus as her Lord and was somewhat surprised when she said yes. What a thrill it was to be able to lead my mom through the sinner's prayer. What an honor and privilege. It was not long after that when she began to suffer more minor strokes. Each one robbed her of part of her memory and resulted in stroke-induced dementia. It was difficult to watch her come to the place where she hardly recognized my wife or me. There came a time when she required round-the-clock supervision, and we knew that we could not provide it for her. It was then we made the decision to place her in assisted living where she could get the care she needed. It was not a difficult decision now. We knew that we had accomplished what God wanted us to do. God was faithful and He knew it would take an extra measure of His mercy and grace. She stayed with us another two years and at least enjoyed a short period of peace and comfort. When the time came, we received a phone call and the staff nurse informed us that her breathing had changed and the prognosis was not good. We needed to come right away. When we reached her bed, we knew that it would not be long. Her breathing was so labored and shallow. As I stood over her, I could not help but feel a sadness. Such a wasted, lonely, frustrating life. There was nothing I could point to that defined a quality life. I thought to myself, "What a waste." Needless to say the Holy Spirit quickly corrected me and said, "Quality of life is not defined by the number of adventures you have been on or the number of friends you have. Quality of life is found in a relationship with the Lord Jesus Christ. Did she or did she not accept Jesus as Lord?" "Why yes she did," said I. Then a quality life she lived," said He. An overwhelming sense of love flooded over me for my mom, and I bent over and kissed her cheek and told her I loved her as she sighed, took her last breath, and went home to be with her Lord.

Is God faithful? Yes, He is. Does He honor His Word? Yes, He does. It took many years; however, He gave me the desire of my heart and I had the privilege of seeing my mom and dad come to know Jesus as their Savior. Is He finished? No, He is not. I did not ask Him only for my mom and dad. I asked for my entire family. The day is coming when all three of my sons are going to be "Davids". That simply means they are going to have a first generation relationship. It is no longer going to be Mom or Dad's God. They are going to have a firsthand relationship with their God. How is it going to happen? That is not my concern. That is up to the Holy Spirit. All I know is that it will happen. Matter of fact, all three of them have in their own unique way experienced the presence of an awesome God.

My middle son had an opportunity to go to Jamaica on a missions trip as a teenager. It was the responsibility of the male team members to move around and keep an eye open for problems. As he came around the corner of the revival tent, he noticed a disturbance up on the hill next to the tent. A group of young rebels had grabbed a young girl and was jostling her around and making threats. Without hesitation or counting the cost, my son made his way into the middle of the group and took the girl's hand. "Come on. You are coming with me," he told her. As he turned to leave, he saw one of the guys holding a knife that was destined for his back. Scott reached up and took the knife from the bewildered boy and placed it on a rock next to him. He then proceeded to share the Gospel with the group and led the knife wielder to the Lord. Later the young man shared with him that he was doing everything he could to plunge that knife into his back and yet he could not do it. It was as if someone or something was holding onto his arm. No matter what he tried, he could not move it. The last report I heard was that young man was a pillar in the local church.

My youngest son heard God speak and place a call on his life while on a missions trip to Australia. God has never, nor will He, remove that call from his life. My oldest son experienced the overwhelming presence of an awesome God at the Charles and Francis Hunter's meeting I shared with you earlier. Will they ever be able to forget what God has done for them? Not a chance. They are great young men, and I believe they still know Jesus. However, there is going to come a day when our parents and my three sons are going to stand arm-in-arm with my wife and me, and together we are going to bow our knees to the King of Kings and the Lord of Lords. How can I be so certain? Because I trust and believe God's Word. I know that He honors His Word. His Word says I shall have the desires of my heart. I desire nothing else. Unrealistic? No! Will it work for you? Yes! God does not have favorites. Paul says in Acts 10:34, "Then Peter began to speak: I now realize how true it is that God does not show favoritism but accepts men from every nation who fear him and do what is right." My wife and I have no special dispensation of grace, nor do we rate any special place in His presence. He will not do anything different in your life than He has done in ours. Simply fall in love with Jesus. Invite Him into your life as your Lord and Savior. Experience the peace and joy and forgiveness that only He can offer. He will not fail you. He cannot fail you because

God Loves the Common Person

What An Awesome God You Are

"Dad, how long are you going to stay up there? Supper is about ready. It is beginning to rain. Don't you think it is about time you come down?"

"Oh yeah! I am on my way. You tell the rest of the guys to get ready. I will be right there."

What an awesome experience that was. I cannot believe I was there for the entire day. I will never forget that day. Let me tell you about it. For several years the Boy Scout Troop my oldest son belonged to had planned a trip to Philmont National Scout Ranch near Raton, New Mexico. As Scout Master, I had agreed to take them if they were able to raise the funds required. They worked hard. The troop held fundraisers, the scouts worked around their neighborhoods doing odd jobs, and they worked together collecting glass and aluminum cans that were recycled. It took several months, however, the day came when thirteen anxious boys, my assistant leader, and myself kissed our families good-bye and climbed aboard the Amtrak train headed for our high adventure.

For many of the kids, the train ride was their first and, in itself, was quite an adventure. When we finally reached our destination, there was a bus waiting to take us to the trailhead where we would begin our journey. We were to spend the next two weeks backpacking in some of the most spectacular country you have ever seen. We would cover 110 miles. After a day of orientation and instruction, we were loaded up with the gear we were to take with us. We had to carry our clothes, our tents, and our food on our backs. The adults and the larger scouts were expected to carry close to 60 pounds while the smaller scouts carried slightly less. All of us were expected to do our part seeing that it would be three days between re-supply stops.

One of the first days out took us up the center of a box canyon. This was not good. It was over 100 degrees and there was no opening on the other end. That could only mean that we were expected to climb out of the canyon. Now wait just a minute. I was carrying 60 pounds. I looked straight up and saw a 400-foot wall. You don't expect me to climb that, do you? Yes they did, and climb I did. Upon reaching the top we were greeted by a beautiful, lush, green valley that led us to one of the most beautiful lakes I have ever seen. It was so still and clear. The reflections of the cliffs in the water were amazing. From there we continued to climb until we came to that night's camp at the base of Mount Baldy. We set up our tents at 9,200 feet above sea level. We were only a few hundred feet below the tree line.

The next day we were to climb to the top of Baldy. It was the highest point at Philmont reaching a height of 12,440 feet.

That night the temperature dipped down to 28 degrees. What an extreme. We started our day in the bottom of the canyon at 100 degrees. The next morning after breakfast the boys were anxious to get started, so off we went. It took about two hours before we came to the tree line. My oldest son was the first to walk out of the woods onto a beautiful pasture-like saddleback ridge. He walked right into the middle of a herd of big horn sheep. They were magnificent animals with massive horns. They simply looked at us and meandered into the woods. We traversed the ridge and found ourselves looking straight up at 1200 feet of shale and rock which separated us from our objective.

This did not look good. "Tell you what, you go on up to the top and I will wait for you here, okay?"

"Nope! We made it this far together. We are not going on with out you, Mr. J."

"You guys don't show any mercy, do you?" So off we went. Rocks. Big rocks Loose rocks. Rocks everywhere. Up and over and around rocks. A 1000 feet to go, 750 feet to go. More rocks. Only 500 feet to go. I was gasping for air. We were 12,000 feet up. There wasn't much oxygen. My lungs felt like they were going to burst. I can't go any further.

"I have had it. You guys go on and I will wait for you here."

"Nope," and they all sat down around me.

"Fellas, you are killing me. Have mercy on an old man." They did not budge. "Okay! Okay! I will try, however, if I die, it will be your fault." Off we went. 400 feet. More rocks. 300 feet. More rocks. Finally only 100 feet left and every part of my body is screaming, "we quit," "we are not going any further!" I sat down and gave up.

"Okay, boys, this is where I give up. I will wait for you here."

"Nope," and they all sat down.

"I don't think I like you guys any more. I think you are trying to kill me."

"Come on, Mr. J., you can do it. We know you can. We are almost there. Please. We do not want to do it without you."

"Okay, okay. You guys go on ahead. I will be right behind you."

"Promise?"

"Yes, I promise."

So off they went. They actually sprinted to the top, and here I was dying. If I ever made it back down, I was going to pound on everyone of them. Only 100 feet. I could do it. I had to do it for the boys. I literally crawled the last twenty feet on my hands and knees, but I made it. I actually made it to the top. As I stood up, I was greeted by the applause and shouts from three different scout troops. Besides my guys there was a troop from Australia and another from Japan. They were all lined up cheering me. I did not know whether I should be elated or embarrassed. I guess it did not really matter. I made it. What an awesome view. We were on top of the world and could see for ever. Mountains everywhere. It was incredible.

Kaboom!!! A huge thunder clap suddenly shook the very ground we were standing on as a brilliant flash of lightning filled the sky. I did not know if God was acknowledging my achievement also or if we were in the middle of a lightning storm. All I do know is that we were on the highest point around and we were not going to stick around and see. Needless to say, we made it down a whole lot quicker than we made it up. Matter of fact, I was one of the first to make it back to camp.

The following day we came upon a small mountain brook. It wasn't very big. We could easily jump across it. It flowed with beautiful, cold, clear water. It would be a perfect opportunity to teach the boys some basic survival skills. You know. Like I was an expert! I took out a small safety pin I carried just in case someone had a problem with their uniform. I tied it on a piece of string and attached the string to a long stick. One of the boys caught a grasshopper that I threaded onto the pin and I let it dance on the stream. To my amazement a six-inch brook trout came out of nowhere and took the bait. I caught a trout. It actually worked. Man, I was a hero at least for the moment.

We had some great times and many wonderful memories over those two weeks.

We finally came to our final campsite. From there we were to pack out to the main road and a bus would meet us, take us back to headquarters, and prepare us for debriefing and departure. For the moment, however, we had two nights on a bluff overlooking a stunning valley that spread out before us for miles. It was beautiful. The next morning we finished breakfast and the boys scattered for their adventures for the day. I walked over to the edge of the bluff and saw this humongous boulder. It was the biggest boulder I think I had ever seen. I looked around for someway to get on the top of it. With the help of a scraggly old pine tree and a few well-placed indentations in the rock, I finally made it. To my wonder and amazement, I found an indentation in the top of the rock that fit me perfectly. I laid back and simply relaxed. I think every bone and muscle in my body was complaining, however, for the moment, it felt so good.

I could see part of our boys off to the left learning to rappel down a 250-foot cliff. That looked awesome. I think I would like to do that, however, my body said no and I simply laid there in the crevice of that huge rock. Chris and the rest of the troop were somewhere down in the valley working at an archeology dig. The museum staff were searching an ancient Indian village for artifacts. My son actually found a museum-quality piece that was placed on display with his name on it.

As I laid there, I was overwhelmed with the beauty and magnificence of God's creation. The cool breeze whistling through the trees. The bright clear sky. The sound of birds singing. It felt as if

God Himself was resting right next to me. I had never experienced His presence like that before. I laid there with tears flowing down my cheeks. It was an incredible experience. Suddenly I noticed off in the distance a small round bright spot in the sky. I became transfixed on a whiff of cloud that began to grow and grow. It took on a life of its own as it created marvelous shapes in the sky. I saw animals, and faces, and birds that would appear and then change into something else. From a humble beginning it grew into a majestic, powerful storm. The wind began to blow. Lightning flashed across the sky. Thunder echoed across the valley. It was spectacular. It was awesome. It was overwhelming. My God, My God. **What An Awesome God You Are !!!**

"Dad, how long are you going to stay up there? Supper is about ready. It is beginning to rain. Don't you think it is about time you come down?"

"Oh yeah! I am on my way. You tell the rest of the guys to get ready. I will be right there."

I will never forget that day. My God revealed Himself to me in a way I did not expect. I was totally swept away with His awesome beauty and power. Now I doubt if you will ever have the opportunity to take a scout troop to Philmont National Scout Ranch.

I doubt if you will ever have an opportunity to climb that rock and experience the hand of God create a tapestry across the heavens before your eyes. You do not have to in order to experience the presence of an almighty God. Look around you. Experience the beauty of His creation. Find Him in the beauty of an autumn tree in all its color. Hear Him in the song of the birds. See Him in the gentleness of the flower as it opens its petals to the warmth of the sun. Experience Him in the giggle of a child. He is all around you. Open your spiritual eyes and see Him. He wants to reveal Himself to you just like He did to me. He loves you. He loves you so much He gave His only Son to die for you. Why then would He not want to show Himself to you. He does. He can and He will if you simply give Him a chance. Why? How can I be so sure? Because I know that I know that

God Loves the Common Person

No, You Just Don't Understand

As I sit here reflecting on the book, I am amazed at the faithfulness of our God. It has taken over half a lifetime to compile. So many good memories mixed with a few that one would just as soon forget. There were wonderful days resting on the "mountaintop" and basking in the glory of His presence. On the other hand, there were many weeks and months struggling through the "valleys" wondering "where are You, God?" As I look back, I have come to realize that it was those times in the valley where God was able to show Himself faithful. I have come to realize that I was not alone in those valleys. He was there. He walked with me and at times literally carried me through them. It was in the valleys where I was shaped and molded into the character I am today. It was in the valleys where this testimony evolved and found its value.

It seems almost anticlimactic to bring this journey to an end. Every good story, like every good journey, must have a conclusion. However, before we can close the book, I must introduce you to one more young couple who have had a very profound effect on my wife and me. They entered our lives when we accepted the pastorate of King Road Christian Chapel in Marine City, Michigan, in the early '90s. They were a pair of young, vibrant, energetic teens who did not have a clue that their journey would have such a tremendous impact on so many people. So, for one last time, sit back and relax and let their story stir your heart.

Hello. My name is Dave and my lovely wife is Pam. We are the very proud parents of four beautiful children. I consider it an honor to be able to share our story with you. It is a journey that began when I accepted Jesus Christ as my savior at the age of fifteen. I was raised in a mainline church that believed their salvation was achieved through a constant repetition of sacraments; however, they never introduced me to Jesus. It was not until a wonderful Christian couple took me under their wings that I met Jesus as my savior, creator, redeemer, and friend. They discipled me and trained me up in the ways of the Lord. I began to attend a little white church with a great big steeple just two doors from my parents' house. It was a place where I was able to grow and flourish under the anointed Word of God.

In 1994 I had an opportunity to go to Argentina on a short-term mission trip with a group of teens from all over the country. It was an experience that totally changed my life and how I viewed the world around me. I met and fell in love with a wonderful young lady while going to that little white church. We were married in 1998 and immediately moved to New York where we attended Elim Bible College in Lima, New York. It is at this point in our lives where our testimony really begins.

While taking a shower one morning I noticed a lump in my left groin that appeared to be growing. My doctor thought it was a femoral hernia and referred me to a surgeon who would be able to correct it. What the surgeon found was not a hernia. He found a swollen lymph gland that he removed and sent away for a biopsy. The results showed that I had non-Hodgkin's lymphoma which is a very dangerous and aggressive cancer. We were forced to move back to Michigan where I began my first round of chemotherapy in 2000. The procedures were moderately effective and resulted in a 95% reduction in the size of the tumor which was maintained over a period of 18 months. There came a point, however, where I needed another round of chemo. By then my body had become resistant to the combinations of chemicals used which meant the doctors had to try something different. They decided to try a drug that was synthesized from the protein of a mouse. Needless to say there was no shortage of jokes from the nurses about cheese, or growing fur, or my nose twitching when I visited the clinic. The problem with this drug is that one out of three hundred patients has adverse reactions to it, and sure enough, I was that one. The head nurse told me to let her know if

I was feeling bad or weird. Now come on, how many chemotherapies feel good? Almost instantly severe cramps in my stomach made it impossible for me to speak. Immediately the doctor injected Benadryl and pain meds in my IV which resulted in a severe drop in blood pressure and I passed out. Four hours later, when I awoke, they asked me if I was ready to continue. For nine hours once a week for the next four weeks I had to endure these treatments which, unfortunately, resulted in only modest gains. The next series of treatments also showed very limited results.

Finally, after several tries with different drug combinations, the oncologist ran out of ideas and had to refer me to the specialists at the University of Michigan who were given permission to try a new experimental treatment that had not yet been approved for general use. The difference between this treatment and the others I had to endure was not in how it attacked the cancer, but the drug was combined with radioactive iodine, which would attach itself to the drug and the drug would transport it to the cancer. I had to spend two weeks literally isolated from my family because of the risk of radiation poisoning. It appeared after everything was said and done that the procedure failed because there was only a 90% reduction in the tumor, and worse yet, it destroyed most of my bone marrow making it almost impossible for my system to produce blood. The only option left was to reset my immune system through a bone marrow transplant.

As we began planning for the transplant, it seemed that there was one roadblock after another. Because of my devastated immune system, I came down with pneumonia which put me in intensive care for nine days. My spleen had to be removed because it was absorbing most of the platelets that were being produced. The biggest hurdle that the doctors had to overcome was finding a suitable donor. The first individuals who were tested were my sisters. The first one failed with a 1 out of 6 on the general matching test. The second one, however, was a perfect 6 out of 6. In the advanced testing she scored a perfect 10 out of 10. The doctors informed us that the odds of having a perfect match between siblings who were not twins was one out of three hundred million. God knew before we were even born that I would have to walk this valley, and no one will ever convince me that, in His providence, He did not provide the miracle I desperately needed. It still amazes me how He moves on our behalf and orchestrates everything so perfectly.

As the time drew near for the transplant, four doctors came into the room and began to argue and debate the best way to proceed. I stopped them and informed them that this was going to be it. There was nothing left. I felt battered, abused, misused and I was not going to endure anything else. I did not care how they approached the procedure, I just knew in my heart that God was either going to heal me or take me home. They all stopped and looked at me as if I was crazy, however, enough is enough. Let's get on with it.

In March of 2006 I went in for the transplant. The actual bone marrow transplant was somewhat anticlimatic. It was nothing more than five days of chemo to destroy the remaining immune system and then a simple transfusion. The seriousness of the situation did not strike me until the second day of chemo when the doctor informed me that there was no turning back now. Either it was going to work or I was going to die. The five days of chemo and the transfusion seemed to go well. The difficulty came in the days following, waiting to see if the procedure was successful. A potentially very serious problem occurred when my nose began to bleed. The transfusion did not have time to take affect yet and I was still extremely anemic. Blood clots appeared and in the process of spitting them out, one became lodged in the back of my throat. I could not lie down. As soon as I would, I would begin to gag and choke. After 34 hours without sleep I was totally exhausted. It took me fifteen minutes to make it to the restroom which was less than 10 feet from my bed. When I finally made it back, I collapsed half on and half off of the bed. I thought this is it. It would be so easy to simply let go and die, however, a still small voice seemed to speak to my spirit. "If your God has brought you through this far, surely He will carry you the rest of the way." A peace that I cannot explain fell on me and a comfort rested upon me like a blanket. I began to thank God, closed my eyes, and fell into a deep, welcomed sleep. When I awoke the next morning I felt a new sense of vigor and energy. The nurses were amazed and said: "You do not look like someone who just came through five days of chemo." A recovery period that should have taken six weeks lasted three weeks. When I went home the doctors were confounded.

It took two and one-half years before the doctors would use the "R" word. Usually after remission the lymphoma is still inside the bones. It is simply kept under control by the new immune system. However, when the doctors checked me over, they were unable to find any trace of the cancer anywhere in my system. They refused to accept the fact that God could heal me so completely. So what did He do to convince them? Pam became pregnant with our fourth child. That truly was a miracle because all of the chemo and radiation should have destroyed my ability to have another child. God doesn't do anything halfway.

I would like to end my story here and say that everything turned out roses, however, I cannot because, in all truth, the story is just getting exciting. Since I lost my spleen, the doctors said I might have problems with fast-moving infections like pneumonia. On March 24th of 2008 an x-ray revealed that I had a minute spot of pneumonia in my left lung. By that evening Pam had to take me to the emergency room because I was having difficulty breathing. The nurse placed me in a wheelchair and that is the last thing I can remember. Another x-ray revealed that my right lung had completely filled with fluid and I was fighting for my life. They had to put me into a medically induced coma and rush me to the University of Michigan Medical Center by helicopter. The local hospital was not prepared to handle the severity of the situation. They thought that it would be just a matter of time and I would die.

I was in that coma for fifty-six days, and Pam did not leave my side for the entire time. Understand, in March she was six months pregnant, she was working full-time, and she was going to school besides raising three children and yet the only time she left me was to go home to shower and catch up on her sleep. She dropped out of school, took a family leave from her job, and made arrangements with members of our church to take care of the children.

What an amazing woman she is. I thank God for her strength, her love and her commitment. I also truly appreciate the members of our church family who took care of our house, paid our living expenses, and took care of the children.

When I reached the UM intensive care unit, the doctors made me as comfortable as they could and informed my wife that I probably would not make it through the night.

Pam would not accept their prognosis and informed them: "You do not understand, our God is not going to let him die. We are going to have a child soon and he will be there to see it born."

"Now young lady, let's be realistic. His system is shutting down. There is little that we can do for him except make him comfortable."

"No, doctors, you truly do not understand. There is a whole army of prayer warriors interceding for him right now. God is going to raise him up and he will be there when I give birth to our child."

What the doctors saw was an impossibility. I had been in a coma for fifty-six days. My weight had gone from 205 down to 172. I had lost all of my muscle mass. The doctors told Pam even if I did survive there would be months of therapy before I could go home. Evidently at a Wednesday service the entire congregation came together and began to intercede for me. They turned their attention to the west toward Ann Arbor and the medical center and began to cry out for my life. I immediately began to improve and I awoke from my coma a couple of days later. At first I was so weak that I could not move let alone get out of bed, however, God was not finished with me and within a few days I was released from ICU and placed in the cardio-pulmonary unit. The first day in the general ward I asked for a wheelchair and had the nurse strap an oxygen tank to the back. It took forty minutes, but I made it to the end of the hall and back. The second day I was motoring all the way around the unit. The third day I stood up and later that day I was walking from one end of my room to the other. Two weeks later by the grace of God and to the doctors' utter amazement I went home just in time to see the birth of Emma Colette. Emma means full of faith and Colette means victorious. What a beautiful child she is. Her name reflects the very heart and soul of our lives together. Never once did we ever give up hope. Never once did we ever doubt God or even ask why. If there is one thought I can leave you with, it is this. Get to know the Lord Jesus Christ in a personal way. He will walk you through any valley you may have to face. He will comfort you and strengthen you. How do I know that? Because He did it for me, and I am no more important than you are. He loves you just as much as He loves me. If He would walk me through such a remarkable journey, He will do the same for you. I take comfort in a Scripture verse found in Philippians 3:13,14 where the apostle Paul declares:

> "Brethren, I count not myself to have apprehended: but this one thing I do, forgetting those things which are behind, and reaching forth unto those things which are before, I press on toward the mark for the prize of the high calling of God in Christ Jesus."

Thank you, Dave and Pam. What an amazing testimony. It would be easy to question God in light of what you just heard. "Why did God have him go through what he did? Why did He wait so long to heal him?" Legitimate questions, I suppose; however, I have never heard either Dave or Pam ask them. Instead they simply gave thanks for God's faithfulness and were content realizing that they had a testimony. Dave told me if one person can come to know Jesus because of what he experienced, all the pain, agony, and suffering were well worth it. Now the question turns to: "How could he possibly endure what he did for so long?" That is simple to answer because both Dave and Pam came to the understanding when they first accepted Christ Jesus as their savior that:

God Loves the Common Person

Conclusion

It is my sincere prayer that the people you have met in these pages have spoken to you, encouraged you, strengthened you, or gave you a sense of hope for your life and your situations. "But Pastor Terry, you do not have a clue to what I am going through." That is very true, however, what I know or do not know is not important to you. The important thing is that you know that you have a God who does understand. It is important that you know you have a God who knows where you are and what you are going through. Jesus came full of love and compassion for you that took Him all the way to the cross on Calvary. He gave His life in order to give you an opportunity to experience forgiveness, joy, peace, and victory over your circumstances. You are no different than I am, or my wife is, or my family is, or those you met in this book. God does not have favorites. Jesus cares about you and your family. He not only wants to help you, He is more than able to do it.

"Well, Pastor Terry, I guess that sounds pretty cool. Everyone you introduced me to saw God take impossible situations and turn them around, and now they are living happily ever after." Whoa now, let's be careful. Yes, God changed the lives of every one you read about. Yes, God changed the lives of those in my family. Yes, God changed my life. He

Conclusion

brought me through some rather dire and potentially dangerous situations. He gave me hope. He forgave me. He gave my life value and a purpose. He placed within me a sense of peace and joy. Realize, however, I still have to live my life on the same playing field you do. Every one you met in this book has to live his life on that same playing field. There are times it is not easy. We are all faced with challenges that seem impossible at times. There are temptations that try to lure us back into the sins we came out of. Whether you are a born-again, Spirit-filled Christian or not, life at times can be a challenge. It is awesome when we find ourselves on top of the mountain rejoicing over a victory or a miracle. I wish I could stay there all the time, however, the reality of the situation is that we live most of our lives walking through the valleys. It is a simple fact of life. Jesus, Himself, informs us in Matthew 5:45, "He causes His sun to rise on the evil and the good, and sends rain on the righteous and the unrighteous."

I was what some refer to as a "tent maker." The Apostle Paul, who traveled far and wide spreading the Gospel, earned his living as a tent maker. For many years, at least until I retired from my secular job, I would preach the Gospel and at the same time earn my living working for a large corporation. It was a challenge at times. I had no difficulty staying busy. There came a time, however, when circumstances began to pile up. The stress and pressure became almost unbearable. God had shown me favor at work, and I was promoted over many who had been there longer than I had. There were jealousies and anger and political haggling from the union. I met obstacles at every turn. At the same time unhealthy attitudes at church began to rear their ugly heads, and I had to deal with gossip and false accusations. Unfortunately, I made some bad decisions. I began to listen to my emotions and I got angry. The stress began to affect my work, my ministry, and my health. My thyroid went wacko because of the stress and I had to have it removed with a radioactive iodine cocktail. Now I am an artificial man taking synthroid every day. I began to suffer from chest pains and had to have a stint placed in one of my arteries near my heart. I came down with Graves disease and the muscles of my eyes began to swell and force my eyes right out of their sockets. I had to endure five sets of surgeries just to keep from going blind. No matter what I tried to do, I could not turn things around. People began to leave the church. I took it personally. "God, where are You? Can't You see what they are doing to me? Why don't you send the lightening and strike them dead?"

I felt betrayed. I felt like a failure. I even questioned whether I was qualified for the ministry. I was convinced that I not only let down those I loved

Conclusion

and respected in the Lord, but I had failed the Lord Himself. I had never experienced a valley so deep and so dark before. It was a difficult time that lasted for several years, and it finally brought me to the point where I had enough. I did not want any more. If this is what Christianity is all about, I do not want it. I am going to change jobs. I am going to leave the ministry. I am going to find a little church where no one knows me and simply sit back and wait for the Lord to come and get me. I give up. Oh boo hoo! Poor me! Well, guess what. Right in the middle of my pity party, the Holy Spirit found a way to get my attention and He spoke to me. It had been a long time since I had heard from Him. I was not really sure He cared any more.

"If that is what you want to do, I am not going to stand in your way. You can walk away if you want to. That is your choice, however, before you do, I want you to answer one question for Me."

"What is it?"

"In order for you to walk away, how much are you going to have to forget?"

"Oh, come on, Lord, that is not fair."

My heart broke. I finally realized what I had been

doing. I had left the Lord out of my circumstances. I had made a choice to listen to my emotions instead of the Holy Spirit. Needless to say I logged a great deal of rug time over that one. What is the point? The point is when we try to live our lives by ourselves and in our own strength, it will invariably lead to failure. It is impossible. That is why I need to constantly remind myself of what the Word of God Says.

> "Even though I walk through the valley of the shadow of death, I will fear no evil, for You are with me. You prepare a table before me in the presence of my enemies. You anoint my head with oil; my cup overflows. Surely goodness and love will follow me all the days of my life, and I will dwell in the house of the Lord forever." Psalm 23:4,5

> "As I was with Moses, so I will be with you; I will never leave you nor forsake you." Joshua 1:5

> "No, in all these things we are more than conquerors through Him who loves us. I am convinced that neither death nor life, neither angels or demons, neither the present nor the future, nor any powers, neither height nor depth, nor anything

else in all creation, will be able to separate us from the Love of God that is in Christ Jesus our Lord." Romans 8:37-39

What awesome promises. What a tremendous lesson I learned in my darkest valley. Through it all, God remained faithful, and He patiently waited until I came to a point where I was able to hear His voice once again. There are still valleys. There are still storms. I will never escape them, and in all reality, I do not want to because, it is in the midst of the storms where He is able to show Himself strong and true. That is where I acquire my testimony.

It was only three or four years ago that my cardiologist informed he was not going to be my primary care physician. He told me he wanted me to have my family doctor give me a complete physical exam. I was feeling great, however, I did what he asked. After my doctor completed the exam, I asked him about a tightness I had had on my right side for many years. It was uncomfortable for me to lie on my back. Could it be scar tissue from an appendectomy I had when I was younger? To be on the safe side, he scheduled an ultrasound. The day after the procedure, the urologist who did it called and said he needed to see me right away. Okay, no problem. It was then that he dropped the dreaded "c" word on me. Cancer! I had a cancerous tumor in my left kidney. My right side was okay.

"Well, doctor, do what you have to do. Let's get it out of there, I have a lot of living left to do."

"That is a strange thing to say. Most men, when I tell them they have cancer, display fear, and fall on their knees and begin to cry. What's with you?"

"What do I have to lose? No matter what happens, I win. I am in a win-win situation."

"What in the world are you talking about? You have cancer and it is not something you take lightly. Don't you understand that it can cost you your life?"

"If you take the cancer out and I am cured, I win because I continue to live and I love life. If I am not healed and I die, I go to be with the Lord Jesus. That is what I have been living for the last thirty some years. How can I lose?"

The next day when I went back with my wife to find out what my options were, the first thing the doctor did was turn to Linda and inform her that I was crazy. Crazy? No! I had come to the point in my life where I could say exactly what the apostle Paul said in Philippians 4:11, "I am not saying this because I am in need, for I have learned to be content whatever the circumstances."

Conclusion

You have heard me say over and over again that I am no one special. I do not have a special dispensation or portion of God's grace. He does not love me more that He loves someone else. What He has done in my life He will and can do in yours. All you have to do is exactly what I had to do, my wife had to do, my children had to do, and all the people you met in this book had to do. We all had to come to the point in our lives where we acknowledged the fact that we were sinners in need of a merciful Savoir. The sin in your life must be dealt with before anything else can happen. It is our sins that separate us from and keep us from our God. You can respond like my mom did so many years ago.

"I am a good person. I have never stolen anything or killed anyone. What makes you think God won't let me into heaven?"

"Mom, it is not a matter of being good. We have all been born with a sin nature. Listen to what the Word of God says."

> "There is no difference, for all have sinned and fall short of the glory of God." Romans 3:23

> "For the wages of sin is death, but the gift of God is eternal life in Christ Jesus our Lord." Romans 6:23

Death simply means separation. It does not mean cease to exist. We are created eternal creatures. We are going to carry on somewhere for eternity. It is either going to be in heaven or hell. It all depends on what we do with the sin issue. I know it sounds hopeless, however, do not cash in the chips yet. There is hope. God has made a provision.

> "But God demonstrated His love for us in this: While we were still sinners, Christ died for us." Romans 5:8

> "Yet to all who received Him, to those who believed in His name, He gave the right to become children of God." John 1:12

I do not believe in coincidences or luck. I believe it was ordained by God that you would have an opportunity to read this book. Take advantage of it. If you have never accepted Jesus as your Savior, or maybe you knew Him at one time and you have turned your back on Him, give Him a chance and say this simple prayer. Mean it and say it from your heart.

> "Lord Jesus. I know that I have sinned against You. I am sorry. Please forgive me. I want You to come into my life and be my Lord and Savior. I promise You

that I will do my best to live for You and to study Your Word. Help me from this day forth to learn to recognize Your voice. Thank You, Lord."

Praise the Lord! Welcome to the family of God. Get ready for an awesome adventure. I want you to do me a favor. Keep this book near you. Let it be a word of encouragement to you when you find yourself in one of your valleys. In the meantime, feel free to contact me at *pastortwj@yahoo.com* . I would love to hear about the difference Jesus has made in your life. God is good, and it is my desire for you to come to the place in your relationship with the Lord where you know that you know that

God Loves the Common Person

Notes

Notes

Notes

Printed in the United States
213338BV00002B/1/P